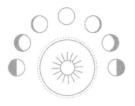

A CIRCLE OF STARS

A guided astrological journey through the lunar
and Celtic wheel of the year

October 2020 - October 2021

by Tara Wild & Jai Gobind

www.acircleofstars.com

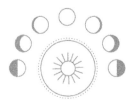

INDEX

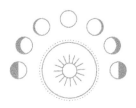

A NOTE FROM TARA WILD

For the past ten years, I have been fascinated with the lives of the ancient Celtic ancestors. This fascination was born from a deep longing to belong to a wider sense of lineage, to connect with the spiritual traditions of my own people, and to remember the ways of the sacred feminine.

If you're of European descent, there's a good chance that you have some or a lot of Celtic ancestry. The Celts were an Indo-European group of tribes with ethnic, linguistic and cultural similarities, and the Celtic lands once stretched over most of Europe before the rise of the Roman Empire. The Celtic culture of old was extremely vibrant with a wide variety of shamanic traditions, rich mythologies, and cultural practices (with important regional differences that have evolved over time and are relevant to a modern understanding of the Celtic traditions). Although these indigenous traditions have been fragmented for the past 2000 years, there are still myths and traditions that remain, providing us with a framework for seeing and experiencing the world through a Celtic lens.

The Celtic path is a living, breathing path, and when we dive into these ancestral practices, we can begin to use our intuition to unearth our own meaningful practices. We can begin listening to the land, the rocks, the trees, who hold the ancient forgotten wisdom, waiting to be remembered.

Something that I have learned through my studies is that the Celts were fascinated with the skies. In writings by the Romans, they speak about the mastery of the Gauls in interpreting the wisdom of the heavens. Sacred sites throughout the Celtic lands are often aligned with the position of the sun on key days (such as the equinoxes and solstices) and there's also significance in the numerology of the stones that align with different astrological cycles. Some of these sites are over 5000 years old which tells us that the ancient Celts were celebrating these sacred cycles for at least that long.

In Ireland, the sacred sites around the River Boyne align with the constellation of 'The High Man' (Orion). The name of the River Boyne itself draws parallels to the Irish word for Milky Way, Bealach na Bó Finne, with 'Bo' meaning cow. Therefore, we can see the River Boyne as the milky cow on earth that parallels the milky cow in the sky. I've included a link to a documentary about the alignment of the sacred sites of Ireland in the Additional Resources section at the end.

The idea for this guidebook came about when I was introduced to Celtic astrology. While I had heard of a Celtic tree zodiac system (by Robert Graves) I always had an intuitive feeling that this system was not quite right, and not truly based on the wisdom of the ancestors. After reading an article by Peter Berresford Ellis (a Celtic scholar I deeply admire) about the misguided notions behind this system, my intuition was confirmed and I started to wonder what true Celtic astrology might have been like.

At the end of the article by Peter Berresford Ellis (published in 1997), he mentions an upcoming book with cosmological and astrological findings based in substantial literary evidence. He didn't mention the name of the book or the author, but I was determined to find it. After reaching out to my community on Instagram about this, someone pointed me in the direction of a book by M.G. Boutet called 'Celtic Astrology from the Druids to the Middle Ages'. I started reading the book and quickly realized that this was the book I'd been searching for.

The book is very in-depth, and certainly worth reading as a companion to this guidebook if it interests you. It is, however, rather complicated, and I wanted to create a more clear and concise way to relate with the information and bring it into my life in an embodied way. I chose one methodology to follow (the Irish Ogham scheme) and began compiling this information into a chart. Through this process, I realized that it would be helpful to create some kind of guidebook that I could come back to again and again with the turning of the wheel of the year. Because Celtic astrology has a lot of gaps - coming from a fragmented lineage - I thought it would also be interesting to cross-reference a more robust astrological system, such as Classical astrology, with the understanding that there would be both similarities and differences between the two systems. It was at this point that I realized that this guidebook, that I desired for myself, would probably be interesting to many others seeking to align themselves with the wisdom of the ancient ancestors and sacred cycles.

At this point, it feels important to say a few things about the presentation of Celtic Astrology in this book. As mentioned, I have chosen the Irish Ogham scheme as the foundation. The way that I have woven the Celtic astrology into the Classical astrology readings is my own interpretation of the information. I do not claim to be an expert in Celtic astrology. I am still learning, still embodying this information, and my heartfelt intention is to bring you along on this journey of discovery.

It also feels important to say that if you don't have any Celtic ancestry, you can still benefit from the wisdom of this book. You can still tap into the divine wisdom of this sacred methodology and appreciate its teachings. In particular, the Celtic wheel of the year provides deep insight into the sacred cycles of the sun and the seasons through the celebration of the equinoxes, solstices, and cross-quarter days.

Another important point is that this guidebook is aligned with the Northern hemisphere, and those in the Northern hemisphere will most benefit from this book because of the way we weave the astrological readings into the seasons of the year. However, you can certainly still garner wisdom from this book if you're in the Southern hemisphere. In relation to the Celtic wheel of the year, those in the Southern hemisphere will want to look to the celebrations that are directly across the wheel, like so:

Samhain - Bealtaine
Winter Solstice - Summer Solstice
Imbolg - Lughnasadh
Spring Equinox - Autumn Equinox
Bealtaine - Samhain
Summer Solstice - Winter Solstice
Lughnasadh - Imbolg
Autumn Equinox - Spring Equinox

Beautiful soul, it's an honor to guide you on this journey. May it help you to remember your own divine connection to the sacred cycles of nature and all of Life. May it help you to walk in the footsteps of the ancestors.

WITH LOVE,
TARA

A NOTE FROM JAI GOBIND

Since the moment Tara Wild reached out to me about co-creating this guidebook I've been exhilarated to be a part of it. My passion is to anchor the light, channel wisdom to the world, and give people hope.

I am an intuitive, writer, songstress, jewelry designer, astrologer and the founder and creator of Eagle Star Yoga LLC, the Eagle Star Sisterhood, Eagle Star Jewels and Channel for Grace. I offer a Moon Goddess Training, an Aquarian Astrology beginners course, and have just finished another online course called Woman and the Moon. I offer astrology webinars, private astrology readings and tarot readings. Through my work, I guide people to connect deeply with their heart space, to find the courage to trust their intuition and align with the healing and sustaining life force of the universe. On my YouTube channel, Channel for Grace, you will find monthly moon, zodiac and collective ascension astrology, as well as new moon and full moon ceremonies for spiritual evolution.

The common thread running through all of the things that I offer is the fact that they allow me to be creative and to be of service to the world. This guidebook is another soulful offering that is filled with so much wisdom from both the ancient Celtic traditions as well as western astrology. It is the best of both worlds. With this book you will have access to symbols and meanings of sacred events that mark our cyclical, astrological and ceremonial calendar of the year.

In the ancient world, people didn't count the days. Instead, they noticed the earth's cycles. They noticed how the sun traveled across the sky, which sometimes brought massive amounts of light, and at other times very little. They noticed that when the sun was strong, the days were hot and fiery and when the sun's light was not as strong, the days were shorter and colder. They noticed that the moon would travel across the night sky. Sometimes it would be fully lit and luminescent, and they noticed that when it was full, the energy was strong and wild.

In the ancient world, people moved with these cycles because they knew that the cycles held wisdom and a deeper knowing about the mysteries of the world they lived in. They could feel how the movement of these two luminaries, the sun and moon, would guide them perfectly every day and every season. The night sky was also something that the ancients watched. They used the constellations to navigate on earth and sea. They noticed that some stars were fixed, while others wandered across the sky.

The original wandering stars they observed where Venus, Mars, Mercury, Jupiter and Saturn. They named these wandering stars and began to notice how the stars affected them, just like the cycles of the moon and the sun. Wisdom comes in many forms and it is my belief that the ancients weren't just observing the sky but also receiving the wisdom transmitted from the energy of these planets and stars.

Astrology was born from the study of the night sky and the cycles of the moon and sun. And many who took the time to listen to the wisdom of the universe received powerful messages that would guide humanity forever. In our modern world, we have forgotten about these cycles because we began to focus all of our energy on organizing time and space, on counting the days, and on expanding our ability to produce more and more, to become more efficient.

We have in essence stepped out of cyclical time and into linear time. But linear time is made up, it's not real. It's a mathematical equation that helps us feel like we are more in control of our lives. But are we really in control? For thousands of years, humanity lived in balance with the cycles and seasons of earth, and now we forget that the moon is even out there, still affecting us whether we know it or not. I wonder if this is why people feel so lost sometimes. In my life, when I began to listen deeply to the voice of wisdom within me, when I began to follow the cycles and celebrate the major shifting points between the equinoxes and solstices, the new and full moons, I began to see that the same wisdom is alive in the cycles of my own body, and in my own life. I began to notice that when the moon is full I feel wild and free, when the moon is new I feel called within. I began to notice that in the summer season, when the light of the sun is strongest, I wish to bring into manifestation all of my inner dreams and desires. I began to see how even the position of the planets and the way they communicate with each other affects us as a collective and as individuals.

There is magic if we choose to see it. People often say that they have to see something to believe it, but I believe it is the other way around. We have to believe it to see it. It's almost as if the universe opens up to you when you open up to it. And that is how wisdom works. When you pay attention, when you listen deeply to your intuition and your inner voice, you hear the universal wisdom speaking through you. The planets, the stars, the moon and the sun are messengers from the universe to humanity. They are our guiding light. They illuminate the collective consciousness, they show us the mysteries of being human, they shine a light into the darkness and they ask us to have faith in ourselves. If we choose to tune in deeply to them we can hear, experience, and embody heaven on earth. As above, so below. The sky is within you, the moon and the stars are our mirror to explore the inner realms of existence. Let them guide you on this magical journey of life.

This book is a dream come true, a light in the dark, an anchor for your Soul. Listen to your inner voice, travel with the cycles of the sun, navigate your inner world with the moon and open yourself up to the magic that lives all around you. As you bring ritual back into your life, as you begin to remember that this ancient wisdom has always lived within you, I hope that you discover your inner universe, your inner light, and that you allow it to shine out just like the sun, just like the stars.

It's an honor to introduce you to A Circle of Stars . . . a bit of magic that was born from a dream, an idea that was planted and allowed to grow through the cycles of time and space, to manifest as powerfully as it is in your hands now. Enjoy and happy journeying!

WITH LOVE,
JAI

ASTROLOGY
INTRODUCTION

PLANETS

CLASSICAL	CELTIC (OLD IRISH)
☉ Sun: your Soul expression	Grian (modern Irish): the three rays; radiant, bright, sunny.
☾ Moon: your emotions	Gaelach: "in phases".
☿ Mercury: your mind	Lct: "bright wanderer" (associated with Lugh)
♀ Venus: your ability to love	Riia: "free star" (associated with goddess Brigid)
♂ Mars: your drive	Goac - "the red"
♃ Jupiter: expansion and spirituality	Tuct - "the messenger" or "traveler"
♄ Saturn: restrictions and authority	Nucturos Uih - "the nocturnal straggler"
♅ Uranus: revolution and individuality	Ean - "liquid/water" (associated with Manannán Mac Lir)
♆ Neptune: dreams and the mystical	Not charted in Celtic astrology
♇ Pluto - death, rebirth, transformation	Not charted in Celtic astrology

NODES

CLASSICAL	CELTIC (OLD IRISH)
☊ North Node	Dragon's head
☋ South Node	Dragon's tail

HOUSES

Please note that some of the houses in Celtic astrology (which are in the Irish Ogham Scheme) are somewhat ambiguous, so I have added my own interpretation in brackets in some places. Please feel free to create your own felt-sense of meaning around these houses.

CLASSICAL	CELTIC
1st House: The house of the Self	Indon: The house of loss, limit and the end result (endings)
2nd House: The house of finances, our relationship to the material world and our values	Lingmen: The house of life, birth, arriving, coming to place (beginnings)

CLASSICAL (CONTINUED)	CELTIC (CONTINUED)
3rd House: The house of communication	Artigatiom: The house of ploughing (setting intentions)
4th House: The house of the home	Eluetia: The house of abundance of goods (material wealth)
5th House: The house of creativity	Uindobios: The house of happiness and bliss
6th House: The house of work and being in the present moment, anchoring the light	Extincón: The house of abundance with the meaning of waxing (this could perhaps be interpreted as the house of abundance of all that is growing/manifesting)
7th House: The house of relationships	Aruos: The house of the striker (could refer to "fire striker" which was a means of lighting a fire, which could be interpreted as ignition/activation)
8th House: The house of change and transformation	Insqiiate: The house of speech and discourse

CLASSICAL (CONTINUED)	CELTIC (CONTINUED)
9th House: The house of spiritual integration	Roudios: The house of the fall (death, destruction)
10th House: The house of career and showing up in the world	Uilia: The house of honesty and will.
11th House: The house of friends and sharing your gifts with the world	Agtate: The house of acts, facts, actions and decisions for action.
12th House: The house of the subconscious mind, bliss and the divine	Ecuodecs: The house of perfect fairness (could be interpreted as harmony and justice)

 SIGNS

You will find descriptions of each of the signs in the Classical, and then followed by the Celtic equivalent. All of the Celtic signs are in the Irish Ogham Scheme.

♈ AIRES (CLASSICAL)

Cardinal fire sign, rules the 1st house, ruled by Mars, the Ram, the warrior, the Fool.

☉ ARB. (CELTIC)

Constellation of the fiery ram. Symbolized by the Ram. Ruled by Goac (Mars). This sign is associated with the seventh house, the house of the striker (could refer to "fire striker" which was a means of lighting a fire, which could be interpreted as ignition/activation). Its hidden meanings include storm, thunder, spark, anvil, and heritage.

♉ TAURUS (CLASSICAL)

Fixed earth sign, rules the 2nd house, ruled by Venus, the Bull, the Empress.

INSCI. (CELTIC)

Constellation of shoots. Ruled by Riia (Venus). This symbol resembles an udder or a heart. This sign is associated with the eighth house of speech and discourse. Its hidden meanings include sincerity and truth.

♊ GEMINI (CLASSICAL)

Mutable air sign, rules the 3rd house, ruled by Mercury, the Twins, the Alchemist, the Magician.

RUIDZUIG (CELTIC)

Constellation of the frisky breezes. Ruled by Lct (Mercury).

Ruidzuig's symbol, similar to classical astrology, has a dual nature which is equal and opposite. This sign is associated with the ninth house of the fall (death and destruction). Its hidden meanings include the cosmic egg, glowing fire, inevitability and death (perhaps alluding to a symbolic or metaphysical death rather than physical).

· ·

♋ CANCER (CLASSICAL)

Cardinal water sign, rules the 4th house, ruled by the Moon, the Crab, the Moon Goddess, the High Priestess.

⚹ IUL. (CELTIC)

Constellation of equity, of the horse. Ruled by Gaelach (Moon). Iul's symbol represents a prancing horse or a person raising their arms to the heavens. This sign is associated with the tenth house, the house of honesty and will. Its hidden meanings include harmony, balance and pleasant demeanor.

· ·

♌ LEO (CLASSICAL)

Fixed fire sign, rules the 5th house, ruled by the Sun, the Lion, the King, Strength.

⚋ OG. (CELTIC)

Constellation of fawns. Ruled by Grian (Sun). Og's symbol represents the lyre/harp, which is also synonymous with the Vega, the alpha star of Lyra known as Uaithne (the Daghda's harp in Irish mythology), which is one of the brightest stars in the summer sky. This sign is associated with the eleventh house, the house of acts, facts, actions and decisions for action. Og's hidden meanings include omen, soothsayer, astronomy and humility.

. . . .

♍ VIRGO (CLASSICAL)

Mutable earth sign, rules the 6th house, ruled by Mercury and Chiron, the Virgin, the Maiden, the Hermit, the Wounded Healer.

⚚ ECH. (CELTIC)

Constellation of the judge. Ruled by Lct (Mercury). This symbol is phallic in nature and is thought to represent fertility. This sign is associated with the twelfth house, the house of perfect fairness. Its hidden meanings include strength, vigor, discreet bounties, fertility, and freshness.

. . . .

♎ LIBRA (CLASSICAL)

Cardinal air sign, rules the 7th house, ruled by Venus, the Scales, the Judge, Justice and balance.

IND. (CELTIC)

Constellation of the ring (representing the wheel of the year). Ruled by Riia (Venus) and Lth (the South Node) as an aspect of Goac (Mars). Ind's symbol is represented by a roe buck, or a deer buck, belonging to the horned God Cerrnunos, lord of the animals. This sign is associated with the first house, the house of the end result (endings). Its hidden meanings include victory and beehive.

SCORPIO (CLASSICAL)

Fixed water sign, rules the 8th house, ruled by Pluto, the Scorpion, the Shadow, Death and transformation.

LII. (CELTIC)

Constellation of the gathering, the sower. Ruled by Goac (Mars) and Ean (the North Node) as an aspect of Nucturos Uih (Saturn). Lii's symbol represents the compass. This sign is associated with the 2nd house, the house of arriving, coming to place and new beginnings. It's hidden meanings include beauty, the living world, and the immortal/eternal.

SAGITTARIUS (CLASSICAL)

Mutable fire sign, rules the 9th house, ruled by Jupiter, the Archer/Centaur, the Traveler, Temperance.

ᚱ RII. (CELTIC)

Constellation of darkness, of the horseman. Ruled by Tuct (Jupiter). Rii's symbol represents a horse's mane. This sign is associated with the third house, the house of ploughing (setting intentions). Its hidden meanings are the treasure and the blessing.

· ·

♑ CAPRICORN (CLASSICAL)

Cardinal earth sign, rules the 10th house, ruled by Saturn, the Goat, the Father, the World.

ᚠ LU. (CELTIC)

Constellation of frost. Ruled by Nucturos Uih (Saturn). Lu's symbol is thought to represent a measuring tool. This sign is associated with the fourth house, the house of abundance of goods (material wealth).

· ·

♒ AQUARIUS (CLASSICAL)

Fixed air sign, rules the 11th house, ruled by Uranus, the Water Bearer, the Prophet, the Star.

⚕ FII. (CELTIC)

Constellation of the cupbearer. Ruled by Nucturos Uih (Saturn). Fii's symbol may represent a warrior figure with arms that have turned into flapping wings (the constellation of the Raven is not far from the constellation of Aquarius). This image is depicted in more detail on an ancient Gallic coin. This sign is associated with the fifth house, the house of happiness and bliss. Its hidden meanings include guide/leader and river/stream.

· ·

♓ PISCES (CLASSICAL)

Mutable water sign, rules the 12th house, ruled by Neptune, the Fish, the Mystic, the Moon.

ᚠ ICT. (CELTIC)

Constellation of coldness. Ruled by Tuct (Jupiter). This sign is associated with the sixth house, the house of abundance with the meaning of waxing (this could perhaps be interpreted as the house of abundance of all that is growing/manifesting). Its hidden meanings include homeland, ethnic home, certainty, truthfulness, chthonic earth (the invisible realm).

RITUAL
INTRODUCTION

There are different ways to create sacred space for rituals. You may already have your own way of doing this, but if you are new to ritual work, here's a guideline that you might like to use.

OPENING SACRED SPACE

Begin by creating a safe and welcoming space. You may wish to create your space outside in the elements, or inside in your home. Make sure to be in a place where you won't be interrupted and where you have privacy. You may want to begin by lighting candles, burning herbs and putting on some music that speaks to your soul.

You can then call in the cardinal directions by turning to each direction and connecting with their energies silently or out loud. For example, you may wish to say, "Spirits of the North, spirits of Earth, Season of Winter, I welcome you into this sacred space. I honor the energies of womb, tomb, soil, silence, mystery and visions. Welcome." Be sure that you know where North, East, South and West are before you begin.

NORTH
Element: Earth
Season: Winter
Themes: womb, tomb, soil, stillness,
silence, mystery, visions

EAST
Element: Air
Season: Spring
Themes: dawn, new beginnings, breath of life,
winds of change, sacred song, possibility

SOUTH
Element: Fire
Season: Summer
Themes: expression, abundance, activation,
creativity, spark of life, transformation

WEST
Element: Water
Season: Autumn
Themes: setting sun, letting go, surrender,
subconscious, dreams, ancestors

You can then invite/welcome in any spiritual guides that you want to connect with. This can include the Celtic deities noted throughout this journal, the wise and well ancestors of your lineage, animal spirits, plant spirits, celestial bodies (the moon, the sun, the planets) and more. Call on protection if you feel it's needed. You then may wish to state your intention for the ritual out loud so that all of Life can hear you.

CLOSING SACRED SPACE

Close the cardinal directions in the order that you opened them, turning to each direction and thanking the energies silently or out loud. For example, you may wish to say, "Spirits of the North, spirits of Earth, Season of Winter, thank you for your wisdom and guidance. I honor the energies of womb, tomb, soil, silence, mystery and visions. Stay if you will and go if you must. Thank you."

Thank and honor the spiritual guides that you have welcomed into the space, sharing your gratitude from the heart.

CREATE A SEASONAL ALTAR SPACE

This is an optional invitation to start an altar to honor the seasons (or perhaps add to an altar that you have already). All you have to do is collect items out in nature that reflect the time of year ~ leaves, seeds, skulls, flowers, herbs, bones, feathers, and more. The idea is that your altar will change as you journey through the seasons (be sure to gift items back to nature when you're finished with them).

It's also good practice to always "ask" before taking something, in which you quiet your mind and ask (in your mind or out loud) the energy of the object or being if you may collect it. You can also explain what you wish to use it for. The idea is that you will "sense" in your body if the object or being gives you a yes or no. If you're not familiar with this practice, just give it a try (and don't worry if you're doing it "right" or "wrong"). It's a beautiful way of honoring the Life that flows through all things.

WINTER
Items: Evergreens and wreaths, feathers, bones, cauldron
Herbs: Mugwort, rosemary, sage, mandrake, wormwood, thyme,
mistletoe, juniper, fir, pine needles, pine cones

SPRING
Items: Seeds, flowers, crystal eggs and painted eggs
Herbs: Angelica, basil, coltsfoot, daffodils, dandelion, primrose, rowan,
nettle, chickweed, apple leaf, snowdrop, daisy, lemon balm

SUMMER
Items: Flower crowns and garlands, white or gold candles, crystals
Herbs: Hawthorne, apple blossom, rose, bluebell, ivy, honeysuckle,
marigold, lilac, violet, tulips, kingcups, meadow-orchids, St. John's Wort,
chamomile, calendula, lavender, meadowsweet, verbena, sage, mint,
elder and roses

AUTUMN
Items: Corn dollies, mead, pumpkins, dried leaves
Herbs: Wheat, corn, barley, heather, sunflower, yarrow, marigold, poppy,
elderberry, scullcap, rosehips, pumpkin seeds, dried apples

SAMHAIN

SAMHAIN

Samhain (Celtic) – All Hallow's Eve – Halloween
Midpoint between Autumn Equinox and Winter Solstice

SAMHAIN PORTAL KEY DATES

Traditional date of celebration: October 31st
Solar Samhain: November 6th, 2020 (3:16pm Pacific)
Lunar Samhain: November 14th, 2020 (9:07PM Pacific)

THEMES

Darkness, ancestors, mystery, the unknown, dreaming, remembering,
regeneration, inner exploration, letting go, intention setting

SYMBOLS

Dark Goddess, burial mounds, drums, rattles,
the Wild Hunt, raven, masks

HERBS, PLANTS & FLOWERS

Mugwort, rosemary, sage, mandrake,
wormwood, thyme

TRADITIONS

Divination, shamanic journeying, ancestral offerings,
masking/disguising/dressing up

ARCHETYPES

Dark Goddess & Lord of the Wild Hunt

In the Celtic calendar, Samhain marks the Celtic new year. This time acts as a portal, a pause, a time of rest and rejuvenation before the rebirth of the sun at the Winter Solstice. This is a time of mystery and magic, visioning and dreaming, and connecting with the unknown. Samhain marks the final harvest of the year and the night of Samhain, known in the modern calendar as Halloween, is a time when the veil between the worlds is thin, when spirits from the Otherworld walk freely among us.

This is an especially important time of the year to connect with and honor the ancestors. Traditional customs include people lighting candles in their windows and in their gardens to guide the spirits of the dead. People would also leave out food for their ancestors and other offerings.

Spiritual leaders would embark on shamanic journeys on burial mounds as a way of communing with the ancestors to receive visions and prophecies, using drums and rattles (which mimic the sound of the ancestors' bones rattling) to experience altered states of consciousness.

As well as the ancestral spirits, there are also many faerie spirits who cross the great divide and make up the 'Wild Hunt', which is a chase led by a mythological figure escorted by a ghostly or supernatural group of hunters passing in wild pursuit. There was superstition that people encountering the Wild Hunt might be abducted to the otherworld or the fairy kingdom, which is why people used to disguise themselves in masks to appear as one of the fae.

The Dark Goddess is the ruler of this auspicious time. She is known as the Cailleach, the Morrigan, Morgana/Morgan le Fey, Cerridwen, Scáthach, and more in the Celtic lands. She embodies the deep mysteries of the unknown and she calls us into a relationship with the birth, death, rebirth cycle that regenerates and gives life. If you have a healthy relationship with letting go and surrendering to the unknown aspects of life, the Dark Goddess will be kind to you. Otherwise, she can use her power to teach us lessons that we've resisted, and it can feel like our sense of comfort and stability is cruelly ripped away from us.

This is a time to dive deep into our inner realms and cultivate a deep sense of resilience, strength and inner truth as we come to terms with what's ready to be let go of. This is a time to experience yourself in the dark womb on the Great Mother, so that you can be transformed and reborn.

ANCESTOR CAKES
SAMHAIN RECIPE

Ingredients:
- 450g plain flour
- 200g caster sugar
- 3 tsp baking powder
- 225g butter
- 28g vegetable lard
- 170g dried fruit
- 2 eggs (beaten)

Sieve together the flour and baking powder. Rub the fat into the flour and mix in the butter. You may need to add a little milk, but the dough should be stiff. Add sugar, beaten eggs, then fruit.
Roll out and cut into rounds to approximately 2cm (¾ inch) in thickness.
Set oven to 180°C (350°F) and bake for 15-20 minutes.

A note from Tara: This is one of my grandmother's recipes. She called them 'Welsh Cakes' because she learned the recipe from the Welsh family she stayed with when she was evacuated from London in WWII. I've called them Ancestor Cakes with the intention of honoring the ancestors at Samhain (see Full Moon ritual on page 35).

OCTOBER 31st, SAMHAIN
FULL MOON IN TAURUS

7:49AM PST

PRIMARY INFLUENCE

Taurus (Classical) - Insci. (Celtic)

THEMES

Electrifying boost of energy
Exploring new things
Kundalini rising
Reflection and adjustments

ASTROLOGY READING

This full moon in Taurus is going to charge us up electrically. With the energies of rest that Samhain invites, we are going to be asked to hold activation in one hand and rest in the other, stretching us to grow and be even more mindful of how we're showing up at this time.

Taurus also invites us to find the comfort and sensuality in life. What do you value? What is important to you? How can you find more security in your life? This energy can help you to reflect on the year gone by, with Samhain marking the end of the Celtic year. It can also help us to get clear about what matters most to us for the year ahead in a grounded, practical way. In Celtic astrology, Insci (Taurus) is connected with speech and discourse, sincerity and truth, inviting us to be in sacred and truthful communion with ourselves at this time.

Uranus is the planet that rules electricity, the kundalini rising, revolution, innovation and the future. With Uranus conjuncting the moon, we will feel a boost of energy to do something we've never done, which will be enhanced by the Samhain portal opening us up to the energies of a new calendar year. We might feel a strong impulse to express ourselves freely and individually. This conjunction can also cause our subconscious emotions to impulsively come out into the open.

Jupiter and Pluto are getting ready for their third conjunction of 2020 which will ask us to adjust to the major financial, economic and structural changes that have occurred since the first conjunction in April of 2020. We will be able to understand more fully how to work with whatever insights and awareness we have gained.

The retrogrades that are present during this full moon are asking us to reflect on how we take action in the world, whether we are truly healing our individual and collective wounds, and if we are integrating lessons that are arising through our subconscious mind. This focus on self-reflection and the subconscious world is also enhanced by the energies of Samhain and the dark time of the year, which calls us into our inner realms.

WHERE IS THIS FULL MOON HAPPENING IN YOUR CHART?

SUN/RISING SIGN	ASTROLOGICAL HOUSE
Aries	2nd house
Taurus	1st house
Gemini	12th house
Cancer	11th house
Leo	10th house
Virgo	9th house
Libra	8th house
Scorpio	7th house
Sagittarius	6th house
Capricorn	5th house
Aquarius	4th house
Pisces	3rd house

Look to page 11 for the definition of each house.

FULL MOON
RITUAL

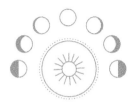

ANCESTRAL HONORING

In this ritual, you will have the opportunity to honor your ancestors in heartfelt ways. There are a few different ways you can do this. You may wish to do one of these options, a few of the options, or all of them.

OPTION #1: SET UP AN ANCESTOR MEMORY SPACE
This is a special space in your home for you to honor your ancestors. You can bring different items to this space such as photographs of recent ancestors, belongings of recent ancestors and family heirlooms, and little offerings such as a cup of mead or the Samhain herbs mentioned above.

OPTION #2: ANCESTOR CAKE OFFERING
You can bake the ancestor cakes (recipe on page 30) and bring one of them into your garden to offer to the ancestors, leaving it under the light of the full moon. You may wish to express your gratitude for the ancestors as you do this.

OPTION #3: ANCESTOR TABLE SETTING
Setting a place at the table for the ancestors is a beautiful practice. While you eat dinner with your family, you can offer the ancestors a plate of food, as though they were sitting with you. You can also have discussions with your family members and children about the ancestors who have passed who are alive in your living memory, honoring them by sharing stories about their lives. At the end of the meal, you can give the food back to the earth, giving thanks for the presence of your ancestors at the table.

NOVEMBER 14TH, LUNAR SAMHAIN
NEW MOON IN SCORPIO

9:07PM PST

PRIMARY INFLUENCE

Scorpio (Classical) - Lii. (Celtic)

THEMES

Clarity
New journeys
Transformation
Preparation for eclipse season

ASTROLOGY READING

While the full moon in Taurus asked us to get clear on our practical priorities for the upcoming year, this new moon in Scorpio is about getting clear on our innermost longings and desires for the year ahead. It's about knowing what we want and planting the seeds to make it happen.

This is symbolized in Celtic astrology by Lii (Scorpio) as the constellation of the sower, which has etymological connections to Samoindon which means "summer's end" and also the word Samhain. Lii (Scorpio) is associated with the second house in Celtic astrology, which is the house of life, birth, arriving, and coming to place, harmonizing with the energies of the new year. Scorpio is the sign that asks us to live life to the fullest and not be afraid of what lies ahead. Having come out of the last of three Jupiter Pluto conjunctions in 2020, we're ready to begin a new journey. With this new moon marking lunar Samhain, these energies also support us in setting intentions and embarking on a new journey.

This new moon is also the last new moon before we enter eclipse season. The energy of Scorpio asks us to dive deep into the underworld and emerge as the Phoenix that rises from the ashes, which is supported by the energies of Samhain, the Dark Goddess, the darkness of winter, and the energies of immortality and new beginnings that Lii (Scorpio) carries. There has been an underlying theme in 2020 of the ending of the old world and the emerging of a new world. This moon is ruled by the planet Pluto which has been spearheading this change since it moved into Capricorn in 2008. Take some time to think about what you want, what kind of dreams you have about the future, and write them down.

WHERE IS THIS NEW MOON HAPPENING IN YOUR CHART?

SUN/RISING SIGN	ASTROLOGICAL HOUSE
Aries	8th house
Taurus	7th house
Gemini	6th house
Cancer	5th house
Leo	4th house
Virgo	3rd house
Libra	2nd house
Scorpio	1st house
Sagittarius	12th house
Capricorn	11th house
Aquarius	10th house
Pisces	9th house

Look to page 11 for the definition of each house.

NEW MOON
RITUAL

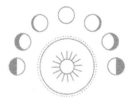

INTENTION SETTING CEREMONY

This is an invitation to go out under the dark moon and do an Intention Setting Ceremony to set intentions for this new year and to release what is no longer serving you.

Begin by creating a sacred space (see page 21 for guidance on this if you're new to ritual work). Place your hands on Mother Earth if you're outside, or the floor if you're inside (connecting to the floor as Mother Earth) and repeat the following words, or something similar, "I release what no longer serves me."

As you're saying these words, focus on releasing anything that is no longer serving you. You may want to move your body as you do this, to release the energy from your body somatically. When you feel that you have released all that you're ready to release, you will then begin to create your intentions for the new year. Begin by reflecting on where you're at in your life right now, what you're visioning for the year ahead, and then write your intentions in a journal.

Once you have your intentions written down, say them aloud so that all of Life can hear you. Really speak from your heart. To conclude the ceremony, you are invited to leave an offering to Mother Earth. Make sure that the offering is biodegradable or some kind of natural object. You may want to give her your moon blood, a piece of your hair, some flowers or a special crystal. You'll end the ritual by closing sacred space (see page 23).

NOVEMBER 30TH
FULL MOON LUNAR ECLIPSE IN GEMINI

(Penumbral Lunar Eclipse, 1:30AM PST)

PRIMARY INFLUENCE

Gemini (Classical) - Ruidzuig (Celtic)

THEMES

Revolution
Mind activation
Moving into the future - the next 6 months
Healing our wounds

ASTROLOGY READING

Eclipse season is a time of powerful and profound change. Eclipses bring in the energy of revolution and upheaval in our lives because it's through these pushes from the universe that we spring into action. A full moon in Gemini is all about activating communication and activating the mind.

This full moon is close to the North Node in Gemini, asking us to find the facts and the truth about what is going on in our lives and to act with our collective future in mind. The eclipse cycle that we're entering is closing off the last eclipse cycle of June and July 2020. We will see some of the issues that were brought up from 6 months ago begin to resolve and come to a conclusion.

These eclipses will activate a new 6-month cycle that will guide us through change and into the future. In Celtic astrology, Ruidzuig (Gemini) is connected with the cosmic egg and death, inviting us to shed our egoic self to liberate our higher consciousness in a radical rebirthing process, which feels potent during this eclipse.

By this point we are also getting really close to the Saturn/Jupiter conjunction at 0 degrees of Aquarius on the Winter Solstice (December 21st 20200. This conjunction will energetically move us into the Aquarian Age. In these times of great change, it's always best to trust our intuition to guide us forward. By this point, Mars will have gone direct after its retrograde in Aries, and we will be able to get moving again towards our goals. This theme is also reflected in Celtic astrology with Arb (Aries) representing the spark, the storm, and the fiery energies of creation.

At the moment of this eclipse, Mars will be trining and sextiling the Nodes, activating our desire to take action towards our divine destiny. The sun in Sagittarius will also be trining Chiron, the wounded healer, who is retrograde in Aries. This full moon lunar eclipse is a call to heal our ego wounds, which is enhanced by the energies of the dark time of year, beckoning us to rest, heal, reflect and grow.

WHERE IS THIS FULL MOON HAPPENING IN YOUR CHART?

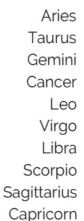

SUN/RISING SIGN	ASTROLOGICAL HOUSE
Aries	3rd house
Taurus	2nd house
Gemini	1st house
Cancer	12th house
Leo	11th house
Virgo	10th house
Libra	9th house
Scorpio	8th house
Sagittarius	7th house
Capricorn	6th house
Aquarius	5th house
Pisces	4th house

Look to page 11 for the definition of each house.

FULL MOON RITUAL

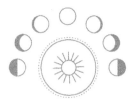

THE CAULDRON OF KNOWLEDGE

In the Celtic tradition, there are three primary energy centers in the body. These three energy centers are called cauldrons. The first cauldron, the base cauldron, is in the belly. This is called the Warming Cauldron, the place of your primal energy, your vital Life force. The second cauldron at the heart space is the Cauldron of Vocation, the place of your heart's calling. The third cauldron is the Cauldron of Knowledge in your mindspace, which is your connection to Source.

In this ritual, you will connect with the Cauldron of Knowledge to activate your mind space and connection with Source. Begin by opening sacred space (see page 21). Get into a comfortable position, close your eyes, and take some deep breaths. Allow yourself to simply be. Bring your attention to your mind space and take as much time as you need to quiet your mind. If a thought comes in, gently release it, coming back into presence.

With your quiet mind, begin to journey deeper into your mind space and imagine that you are visiting the Cauldron of Knowledge in your mind. What does this energy center look like? What does it feel like? When you have become acquainted with this cauldron, ask yourself, what nourishes this cauldron of energy? What depletes this cauldron of energy? As you continue to connect with this cauldron, see if you can open yourself up to experience your direct connection with Source. Stay in this space for as long as you like. When you feel complete, take some time to write in your journal about your experience. Close sacred space (see page 23).

DECEMBER 14TH – NEW MOON
TOTAL SOLAR ECLIPSE IN SAGITTARIUS

8:17AM PST

PRIMARY INFLUENCE

Sagittarius (Classical) - Rii. (Celtic)

THEMES

The return of hope
Freedom
Fiery revolutionary passion
Divine course

ASTROLOGY READING

This total eclipse is going to be POWERFUL! The peak of this eclipse is actually passing over a small town in Argentina called Esperanza. Esperanza means "hope" and this eclipse is here to bring us hope. Although it's a South Node eclipse, which means there are a lot of past life karmic things that come up to be resolved and past issues that need to be dealt with, it's the kind of eclipse that will remind us of the future that we're building.

A Sagittarius moon is all about freedom, independence, exploration, and divine curiosity. It has to do with higher education, finding the Truth, and connecting deeply to your faith. While the South Node in Sagittarius has been restricting travel, and creating situations where we are falling into belief systems that are false, this eclipse will begin to change the course of history. In Celtic astrology, Rii (Sagittarius) is connected to the dark horse, the archer, setting intentions and blessings. If we're able to master the Shadow aspects of ourselves and set true intentions with faith and focus, we'll reap the rewards, which feels very potent during this eclipse.

With this new moon solar eclipse conjunct Mercury and trine the planet Mars, our higher mind will be activated and we will look for ways to resolve what comes up both individually and collectively. The trine to Mars will give us the fiery passion to go for what we believe in. With so much fire energy in this chart we have to remember that we are still in revolutionary times yet somehow, I think that on this day we will begin to feel our faith restored in humanity. We will be reminded that what lies ahead is amazing and we just have to stay on our divine course.

WHERE IS THIS NEW MOON HAPPENING IN YOUR CHART?

SUN/RISING SIGN	ASTROLOGICAL HOUSE
Aries	9th house
Taurus	8th house
Gemini	7th house
Cancer	6th house
Leo	5th house
Virgo	4th house
Libra	3rd house
Scorpio	2nd house
Sagittarius	1st house
Capricorn	12th house
Aquarius	11th house
Pisces	10th house

Look to page 11 for the definition of each house.

NEW MOON
RITUAL

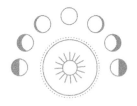

JOURNALING PRACTICE

This eclipse is going to be powerful. Take some time to simply be, and feel all that wants to be felt. Here are a few journaling questions for you to engage with as you're in this reflective process:

What needs to be resolved at this time?

How can I take steps to resolve what needs to be resolved?

Are there moments in my life when I feel a deep sense of faith and trust?

How can I cultivate more faith and trust in my life?

WINTER
SOLSTICE

WINTER SOLSTICE

Midwinter - Yule - Alban Arthan (Druid) - Christmas (Christian)
The shortest day and longest night of the year

WINTER SOLSTICE PORTAL

Solstice: December 21st, 2020
Solstice portal: December 20th - December 22nd

THEMES

Rest, rejuvenation, pause, inner reflection,
rebirth, sovereignty

SYMBOLS

Womb and tomb, light and shadow,
rebirth of the sun, wheel of life

HERBS, PLANTS & FLOWERS

Mistletoe, juniper, fir, pine needles, pine cones

TRADITIONS

Divination, visioning, intention setting,
making Yule logs

ARCHETYPES

The Crone & the King

In Irish, the winter solstice is known as 'An Grianstad' which means 'the sun stop' as the sun literally appears to stop in the sky, after which the days begin to grow longer. This festival is first and foremost a celebration of the rebirth of the sun (later known as the birth of the Son of God in the Christian tradition). At the ancient site of Brú na Bóinne in Ireland (also known as Newgrange) the sun shines into the darkness of the burial mound through a window above the entrance. The rays of the sun represent the penetrating energies of the divine masculine, and the darknes of the burial mound represents the womb of the divine feminine.

We not only celebrate the return of the sun at this time, but also the wisdom of darkness. Modern society tends to fear or misunderstand darkness, but it's from darkness that we came (from the dark of the womb) and to darkness we'll return (into the tomb and soil of the earth).

Those on a spiritual path also know that our greatest transformation comes from working with our Shadow/our darkness. The solstice is therefore a time for rest, divination, visioning, dreaming, and intention setting.

The womb, the soil, the burial mounds, the cauldron, the long dark of the night . . . this is the wisdom we honor on this day, alongside the solar codes of the sun/divine son returning as King.

This is a time to honor the Cailleach, the Crone, the Old Wise Woman of the World, who keeps things in balance. She is a fierce voice of nature, a gatekeeper of cycles. She is also a bestower of sovereignty to those who are worthy. We also celebrate the Holly King at this time, who is the ruler of the waning half of the year when the days grow shorter. He is crowned on Winter Solstice and then dies so that the Oak King can be reborn, who is the ruler of the waxing half of the year when the days grow longer.

Traditional customs of decorating the home with evergreens has lasted well into modern day, with door wreaths representing the wheel of Life. Mistletoe was traditionally used for sacred and magical purposes, and was ceremonially used to cure diseases, provide spiritual protection, bring good luck, and aid fertility. According to the Anglo-Saxons, kissing under the mistletoe was connected to the legend of Freya, goddess of love, beauty and fertility. This is where the tradition of kissing under mistletoe first began.

YULE LOG WINTER SOLSTICE RECIPIE

Cake ingredients:

- 60g (¼ cup) coconut oil
- 250 ml (1 cup) unsweetened almond milk
- 1 tbsp apple cider vinegar
- 1 cup maple syrup
- 1 tsp vanilla extract
- Pinch of salt
- 150g (1 ¼ cup) almond meal
- 150g (1 ¼ cup) plain flour (substitute for gluten free flour mix if desired)
- 2 heaped tsp baking powder
- ¼ tsp baking soda
- 50g (½ cup) cocoa powder
- ¼ tsp nutmeg
- 1 tsp cinnamon
- ½ tsp cardamom
- 1 cup of dried cherries (softened)

Frosting ingredients:

- 150g (1 cup) raw cashew nuts, softened
- 225g (1 ⅓ cup) cooked peeled chestnuts
- 9 tbsp maple syrup
- 120ml unsweetened almond milk
- 4 ½ tbsp cocoa powder
- 1 ½ tsp vanilla extract
- Flaked almonds (for decoration)

CAKE INSTRUCTIONS

Soak dried cherries in hot water for 15 minutes in water, or in brandy overnight (at least 4 hours). Soak cashew nuts in hot water for 15 minutes. Preheat oven to 350°F (180°C).

Melt the coconut oil in a pan. Once melted, put into a mixing bowl and add the almond milk, apple cider vinegar, maple syrup, vanilla, salt, and almond meal.

Stir in the flour, baking powder, baking soda, cocoa powder, nutmeg, cinnamon, and cardamom. Mix well. Add more almond milk if it's too dry.

Drain the softened cherries, roughly chop, and add them into the mix.

Line a baking tin with parchment paper. Put a splash of oil in the bottom of the pan to stop the parchment paper from slipping. (I use a 9" long, 13" wide, 2" deep baking tin.)

Transfer the mixture into the baking tin.

Bake for 20 minutes until risen and an inserted skewer comes out clean.

Take it out of the oven and remove from the pan by inverting onto a flat board that's bigger than the pan (such as a long cutting board).

Remove the parchment paper and allow to cool for 10 minutes until it's hand hot.

Lay a clean cloth kitchen towel onto the cake and gently roll in into a spiral. The kitchen towel temporarily takes the place of the frosting until it cools completely (at a later stage you will take out the towel and replace it with the frosting). You will want to hold the cake quite firm as you roll it, and you may want to use a large spatula to help bend it. Don't worry if you squish the cake a little bit, this can actually help to create the roll shape.

Let the cake cool completely in the towel for an hour.

FROSTING INSTRUCTIONS

Drain the cashews and put them into the food processor with the chestnuts, maple syrup, unsweetened almond milk, cocoa powder, and vanilla extract.

Blend until completely smooth. You may need to blend it a few times. If the frosting isn't thick enough, add more chestnuts.

You now need to gently unroll the cake and remove the kitchen towel. Don't worry if the cake is cracked and squished in places.

Spread the frosting over the top side of the cake, making sure to fill all of the cracks.

Use your hands to roll the cake back into the spiral shape. Cut off the ends of the cake to level them, then transfer the cake onto a serving dish.

Use a spreading knife to spread the frosting over the entire cake.

Decorate with flaked almonds.

WINTER SOLSTICE ASTROLOGY
DECEMBER 21ST

PRIMARY INFLUENCE

Aquarius (Classical) - Fii. (Celtic)

THEMES

An auspicious new beginning
Aquarian Age energies arrive
Moving into the future of humanity
Determination and commitment

ASTROLOGY READING

Astrologically speaking, this is the most auspicious day of 2020. Every 20 years, the planets Saturn and Jupiter come together in a conjunction that sets up the energy for the next 2 decades. On this day, we will see Saturn and Jupiter come together at 0 degrees of Aquarius, exactly on the Winter Solstice, the exact moment that the sun enters the sign of Capricorn.

Because this conjunction is happening at the cusp of Capricorn/Aquarius it will be a very strong transit. Both Jupiter and Saturn love being in Aquarius. In fact, Saturn is the traditional ruler of Aquarius so it's at home in this zodiac sign. Having Saturn dignified during this conjunction strengthens its powers. Jupiter expands everything it touches so in Aquarius, he will expand our minds and bring us to the highest levels of awareness possible.

This conjunction is the ultimate doorway to success and achievement. The energy of Aquarius will inspire us to collectively and individually seek new and innovative ways to succeed, and will activate massive revolutions in the self and in our sphere of understanding. This powerful blast of Aquarius energy will completely change the paradigm of our reality. Aquarius literally represents change. In Celtic astrology, this is represented by the lessons of the river which are associated with Fii (Aquarius), where we are always being asked to flow, to grow, and to change course. If we try to grasp onto the river bank, onto what we know, we will ultimately suffer. But if we let go and trust, we will be rewarded.

On this day, change is here on a massive scale. We will feel like we are taking off into the future, starting from this point on in our lives.

This conjunction is closing off the cycle from the conjunction Saturn and Jupiter had in 2000 and beginning a completely new cycle focused on the future of humanity.

This, my friends, is the beginning of the Age of Aquarius. This is the first of many Aquarius transits and Aquarius energies that we will see in 2021 and years to come. 2020 has been all about seeing the old structures of government and life collapse, it has been about watching the tower fall, about learning how to be patient, and setting ourselves up for success. 2021 is the year that many doors/opportunities will begin to open, where there will be much more flexibility and an exciting energy in the air as the higher vibrational frequencies from these powerhouse planets launch us forward.

On this day, the sun will be conjunct Mercury as it enters Capricorn, keeping our thoughts and ideas on ambitious desires for success, setting us up to plan our goals with determination and commitment. The moon will be conjunct Neptune which will activate our higher mind, intuition and psychic powers to channel information for the beyond. Saturn and Jupiter will be squaring Uranus which is the planet of revolution, and rules the sign of Aquarius. Get ready for big changes, unpredictable shifts and amazing new doors to open. This day is a powerful portal towards the future, towards the Aquarian Age.

DECEMBER 29TH
FULL MOON IN CANCER

7:28PM PST

PRIMARY INFLUENCE

Cancer (Classical) - Iul. (Celtic)

THEMES

Home and family
Healing familial and relationship karma

ASTROLOGY READING

After the powerful eclipses, the powerful Winter Solstice, and our emergence into the a new dimension with the Age of Aquarius, we are now in a new world. It's here that we arrive at a full moon in Cancer that wants us to focus on the realm of home and family.

What's important to us when it comes to feeling at home? What kind of people do we want to surround ourselves with? This moon will be opposing Mercury which can cause a bit of communication confusion but with Chiron T-squaring the full moon we are also being called to heal and to face our deep-seated wounds relating to our family and home environment.

Neptune will be T-squaring the Nodes on this day as well, calling us to see where we have fallen victim to illusion and deception in our lives. At the same time, Venus will be conjunct with the South Node. If you understand that the South Node is about the karmic past, then you realize that seeing Venus (a benefic planet that usually likes to bring in happy and abundant energy) conjunct with the South Node will make her feel trapped and not able to provide her usual feel-good energy.

Venus conjunct the South Node is about dealing with relationship karma. With Venus squaring Neptune, this will get exacerbated, and this is the kind of transit that can cause relationship problems. It's no coincidence that the moon in Cancer and Chiron will call us to heal the relationships of those we're closest to, especially at home.

In Celtic astrology, lul (Cancer) is connected with honesty, harmony and balance, which can aid us in navigating the healing that's being called for. The truth is that in order to move into a new world, the collective healing that needs to happen is deeply connected to our own personal and internal healing.

WHERE IS THIS FULL MOON HAPPENING IN YOUR CHART?

SUN/RISING SIGN	ASTROLOGICAL HOUSE
Aries	4th house
Taurus	3rd house
Gemini	2nd house
Cancer	1st house
Leo	12th house
Virgo	11th house
Libra	10th house
Scorpio	9th house
Sagittarius	8th house
Capricorn	7th house
Aquarius	6th house
Pisces	5th house

Look to page 11 for the definition of each house.

FULL MOON RITUAL

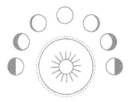

HEART OF THE HOME

In this ritual, you are invited to cultivate healing energy in your home, with you embodying yourself as the heart of the home.

Begin by opening sacred space (see page 21). This ritual is best done in your home. Take some time to connect with the energies of the moon. Feel the way that the moon moves the tides, and the waters of your body. Place your hands on your heart, close your eyes and take some deep breaths. Feel your heartbeat. Bring your full attention to this space, letting all thoughts dissolve away until you are completely present to your heart.

Begin to feel your heart space as a flowing river that flows from behind you, through your heart, and then out in front of you, as though the waters are pouring out of your heart space. Place your attention and intention towards infusing these sacred waters with your love. Feel your heart opening more and more, allowing these watery, lunar energies of love and healing to flow through you. Feel these energies traveling into every area of your home, until the space is vibrating with codes of love and healing.

When you have finished this, you can reflect on the question, "How can I use my voice to bring more heart into my home?" You may wish to write down any reflections in your journal. Finish by closing sacred space (see page 23).

2021

JANUARY 12TH
NEW MOON IN CAPRICORN

9:01PM PST

Capricorn (Classical) - Lu. (Celtic)

THEMES

Building our future
Cleaning up the mess
Destruction of old patterns and structures
Finding the patience to innovatively move
forward in life

ASTROLOGY READING

Mars has officially finished its transit through his ruling sign of Aries and moved into Taurus and as a result, we will feel a big relief. Mars in Aries has tested our patience, turned on our drive, caused conflicts to arise, and activated our fighting spirit . . . but it has left us feeling like, so who's gonna clean up the mess?

If you consciously moved with Mars in Aries towards the higher expression of the Sacred Warrior, you should've been able to move forward with what you wanted to do. But if you fell under the spell of an innocent, ignorant, and impulsive Aries, you may have a mess to clean up in your life. In Celtic astrology, Arb (Aries) holds the energies of the storm, also ruled by Goac (Mars), and can either be a divine storm in our lives which brings new opportunities and ideas, or it can be the kind of storm that destroys everything in its path.

This moon is not necessarily going to be an easy one because it will be conjunct Pluto. As a new moon, the energies are about setting intentions towards a successful future. However, with Pluto (God of the underworld) conjunct this moon, it will feel a little shaky. Pluto likes to destroy things, cause towers to fall, and transform our lives. In short, transits are never easy with Pluto. The sun in Capricorn needs to be recognized for their status, which is also reflected in Celtic astrology with Lu (Capricorn) being symbolized by the measurement of material wealth and abundance. While the moon in Capricorn restricts its emotions, Pluto in Capricorn destroys old patterns to make room for a whole new world.

These three planets together are about emotional intensity, power, and control dynamics. With so much pressure from Pluto in Capricorn, some may feel like giving up but this is not the time to give up.

To add to this intense energy, Uranus will be squaring Saturn, Jupiter and Mercury, who are all in Aquarius. With these three planets being in the ruling sign of Uranus, we will see Uranus activating its power through them. This means that Saturn will help us to find innovative ways to move forward into the future. Jupiter will expand Saturn's power to make this happen, and Mercury will give us access to our higher mind.

The last Mars square to Saturn is happening the day after this new moon, so tensions are still high, but with Mars in Taurus we are going to experience this transit completely different than when Mars was in Aries. We will be much more calm and patient with Mars in Taurus, giving us space to pause and figure out what we really want to put our energy into.

WHERE IS THIS NEW MOON HAPPENING IN YOUR CHART?

SUN/RISING SIGN	ASTROLOGICAL HOUSE
Aries	10th house
Taurus	9th house
Gemini	8th house
Cancer	7th house
Leo	6th house
Virgo	5th house

SUN/RISING SIGN (CONTINUED)	ASTROLOGICAL HOUSE (CONTINUED)
Libra	4th house
Scorpio	3rd house
Sagittarius	2nd house
Capricorn	1st house
Aquarius	12th house
Pisces	11th house

Look to page 11 for the definition of each house.

NEW MOON RITUAL

JOURNALING PRACTICE

This new moon is going to be intense. Be sure to take care of your needs and spend some time alone in quiet reflection. Here are some journaling questions for you to explore:

In what areas of my life can I take more personal responsibility?

In what areas of my life do I need to bring more patience?

Are there any areas of myself or my life that I need to forgive, and is there anyone that I need to apologize to at this time?

JANUARY 28TH
FULL MOON IN LEO

11:16AM PST

PRIMARY INFLUENCE

Leo (Classical) - Og. (Celtic)

THEMES

All systems go!
A window of opportunity
Sun/Jupiter day - auspicious energies
Intensity in relationships

ASTROLOGY READING

This day is a day to celebrate because we officially have all planets moving direct! Finally, after months and months of retrogrades we find ourselves at a beautiful auspicious day to celebrate this phenomenon. But it won't last long because Mercury will be going retrograde on January 30th for a short visit (through February 20th).

After this Mercury retrograde, all planets will be direct for about 3 months until Pluto goes retrograde at the end of April 2020. It seems like this window of opportunity opens just in time for this full moon, so we better take advantage of it! This energy is enhanced by the auspicious energies that Og (Leo) brings, who is connected with omens, soothsaying, and multidimensional frequencies, and who desires to shine brightly, just as Uaithne (Lyra) shines as one of the brightest stars in the summer sky (represented by Og's symbol).

With the sun, Jupiter and Saturn in Aquarius, this is serious business in regards to looking at the future of humanity and towards our own individual future. In Celtic astrology, Fii (Aquarius) is the constellation of the cupbearer, invoking symbols of the womb of creation and the Cauldron of Regeneration, where all things can be transformed and reborn. This sign invites us to embrace our leadership to be rewarded with the transformational qualities of the Cauldron of Regeneration (like the Holy Grail) which leads to spiritual fulfillment, happiness and bliss. The sun (our Soul expression) yearns for independence, freedom and individuality. Saturn in Aquarius will try to find ways to organize this, and Jupiter will expand these energies.

But we also have to remember that the moon in Leo desires to feel seen, valued and wants to shine brightly, too. This duality is the energy of the king versus the people, so even though the moon might want to be the center of attention, more energy will be drawn towards the sun in Aquarius to focus on community and group effort.

When the Sun and Jupiter are in exact aspects to each other, we call this a Sun-Jupiter day. Sun-Jupiter days are very auspicious. They are good for starting things or initiating projects. With a full moon happening at the exact time, the effect of this day will be exponentially magnified. With Mars in Taurus conjunct Uranus, we will feel a drive to build something and manifest our dreams into reality.

The T-square on this day (from Uranus and Mars to the full moon) will create tension that needs to be resolved, but will also offer a lot of energy and drive to resolve them. The other important aspect on this day is the exact conjunction between Venus and Pluto at 25 degrees of Capricorn. In terms of relationships, this can create intense desires and passion, but Capricorn will create a little resistance here and not everyone will feel comfortable to express it.

WHERE IS THIS FULL MOON HAPPENING IN YOUR CHART?

SUN/RISING SIGN	ASTROLOGICAL HOUSE
Aries	5th house
Taurus	4th house

SUN/RISING SIGN (CONTINUED)	ASTROLOGICAL HOUSE (CONTINUED)
Gemini	3rd house
Cancer	2nd house
Leo	1st house
Virgo	12th house
Libra	11th house
Scorpio	10th house
Sagittarius	9th house
Capricorn	8th house
Aquarius	7th house
Pisces	6th house

Look to page 11 for the definition of each house.

FULL MOON RITUAL

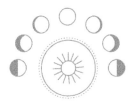

PROJECT ACTIVATION

With the energies of this full moon, this is a great time to start a new project. If there's been a project that you've been putting off or wanting to get to for some time, now is the moment to activate it. Projects that serve a greater purpose will feel especially potent at this time. Before you start this ritual, decide which project you're going to activate.

Begin by opening sacred space (see page 21). State your intention aloud of what project you are going to activate in this ritual, and what the project means to you.

With a large piece of paper, spend some time getting all of your ideas about the project onto paper. Then write down your initial steps for starting the project, and make a plan to execute them before the next new moon.

Finally, spend some time in quiet reflection with your eyes closed, feeling if there are any spiritual or ancestral guides who want to support you in activating this project. Finish by closing sacred space (see page 23).

After this ritual, you may want to spend some time on your first action steps to get the project going.

IMBOLG

IMBOLG

Imbolg/Imbolc (Celtic) – Candlemas (Christian)
Midway point between Winter Solstice and Spring Equinox

KEY IMBOLG PORTAL DATES

Traditional celebration date: February 1st
Solar Imbolg: February 3rd, 2021 (7:16am Pacific)
Lunar Imbolg: February 11th, 2021 (11:06AM Pacfic)

THEMES

Awakening, creativity, initiation, intuition,
reclamation, erotic innocence, healing

SYMBOLS

Brigid, Brigid's Cross, candles, sacred springs
and wells, sheep, milk

HERBS, PLANTS & FLOWERS

Angelica, basil, coltsfoot, daffodils,
dandelion, primrose, rowan

TRADITIONS

Candle/lantern processions, pilgrimages to sacred springs
and wells, making Brigid crosses, divination, writing poetry,
singing songs, crafting and storytelling

ARCHETYPE

The maiden

Imbolg means 'in the belly', a time when the Celtic Isles begin to feel the first whispers of spring . . . when from the belly of the earth, deep in the soil of our souls, we feel the quiet call to turn our attention outward with gentleness. Imbolg is the time when the sheep are pregnant and are beginning to lactate with milk. This celebration is marked with the lighting of candles and processions of lanterns to mark the growing power of the sun. This is also a time for healing and awakening the deepest and truest aspects of ourselves.

Imbolg is the celebration of Goddess Bridget/Brigid/Bride/Brigantia. Goddess of the three faces. Goddess of fire. Goddess of healing. Goddess of the sacred wells. Goddess of hearth and home. She is a triple goddess. Her aspects are the poet, the healer, and the blacksmith, and also the mother, the maiden, and the midwife.

Her combination of fire and water elements create great magic that can aid us in our journey of inspiration, creativity, healing, and transformation. She holds both the maiden and mother archetypes, and is the ruler of the warm half of the year. At Imbolg, which marks the very beginning of spring, her energies return to the land after being in the depths of winter.

There are some interesting similarities between Brigid and Mother Mary, who are both celebrated at this time (Candlemas celebrates the 'Purification of the Blessed Virgin Mary'). The ancient ancestors saw virginity as something very different than what is perceived today. The word virgin simply meant an unmarried woman, connecting virginity to the powerful aspects of the maiden who is initiated by her own sexual innocence and awakening.

As keeper of the Sacred Fire, Brigid helps to awaken the divine spark of inspiration within us, and her waters help our creativity to flow. Traditionally this is a time for storytelling and poetry, which are other aspects of Brigid's sacred medicines. These creative energies can also help us to connect with our intuition, the wisdom of our dreams, and our deeper selves. This is also a time for healing with Brigid's sacred waters, and connecting with her sacred wells.

Above all, this is a time to reclaim the lost parts of ourselves, shed limiting beliefs and conditioning, and bring forward the wisdom we've cultivated from the winter months. It's a time to ask ourselves, "Who am I becoming? What's awakening in me?"

SPICED HONEY MILK & SHORTBREAD IMBOLG RECIPE

Spiced honey milk ingredients:
(2 servings)
- 600ml milk (can use oat milk or almond milk if dairy free)
- 2 tsp honey
- 1 tsp of cinnamon
- 1/2 tsp cardamom
- Pinch of nutmeg

Shortbread ingredients:
- 350g plain flour
- 225g unsalted butter at room temperature
- 110g caster sugar

SPICED HONEY MILK INSTRUCTIONS

Simply combine all the ingredients together and warm on the stove. Remove from the stove just before the mixture begins to boil.

SHORTBREAD INSTRUCTIONS

Blend together the butter and sugar, then add the flour to form a finely formed breadcrumb-like mixture (you may want to do this in a food processor). Roll out into a 2cm (¾ inch) thickness and cut into small circles. Place in the fridge for 30 minutes to completely chill the mixture.
Set oven to 180˚C (350˚F) and bake for 15-20 minutes.

IMBOLG ASTROLOGY
FEBRUARY 1ST

PRIMARY INFLUENCE

Aquarius (Classical) - Fii. (Celtic)

THEMES

Focusing on the future
Competition
Creative activation

ASTROLOGY READING

This day is one of the first days of 2021 where we will start to see the powerful energy of Aquarius coming together. We will have the sun, Venus, Mercury, Saturn and Jupiter all in Aquarius making a stellium in the sky. A stellium is three or more planets in the same sign. It basically means that there is heavy Aquarius energy affecting us.

What is even more interesting is that this stellium is part of a grand trine in air between all these planets in Aquarius, the North Node, and the moon in Libra. This grand trine in air will activate our intellect, turn on our higher mind and help us focus all of our energy on the future and towards the North Node (which is the symbol of destiny and humanity's collective purpose). In Celtic astrology, the connection between Fii (Aquarius) and Ind (Libra) will invite us to activate our leadership in ways that bring us into deep communion with the circle of life, where endings are always falling into new beginnings.

The sun will be exactly squared Mars at 13 degrees, creating an aura of competition and drive. Saturn will be exactly sextiling Chiron at 5 degrees, making sure that we continue to be inspired to do the inner work that is needed to keep moving forward. With Mercury having just gone retrograde in the sign of Aquarius, we will begin to reflect on what has worked, what hasn't, and what needs to be changed in regards to our plans for the future (both collectively and individually).

What's most intriguing about the astrology of this day and the celebration of Imbolg is the fact that Fii (Celtic) and Aquarius (Classical) are both represented as the water bearer in the sky, just as Brigid is the Goddess of the sacred wells. Although in classical astrology Aquarius is an air sign, Aquarius is the one that holds the magical waters of life in his hands, and the one who nourishes us with this powerful life force.

On this day, we celebrate Brigid's waters that help us to connect with our creative flow. Simultaneously, we see massive Aquarius energy in the sky, who in essence holds the waters of creativity as well. These sacred waters are poured out towards humanity, activating our creative powers.

FEBRUARY 11TH, LUNAR IMBOLG
NEW MOON IN AQUARIUS

11:06AM PST

PRIMARY INFLUENCE

Aquarius (Classical) - Fii. (Celtic)

THEMES

Independence and freedom
Love, harmony and happiness
Falling in love

ASTROLOGY READING

When we arrive at this moon we are going to see another epic stellium in the sky! On this day, the Aquarius stellium includes the sun and moon, along with Mercury, Venus, Jupiter and Saturn. This holds similar energies to Imbolg, but now the moon has caught up with this stellium.

These planets, especially Jupiter and Saturn, are big players in the astrological wheel so they pull a lot of energy towards them. When the energy of Aquarius is activated, we start to think with our higher mind. We start to revolt against authority. We desire to join together with other people in groups, and we begin to desire independence and innovation. In Celtic astrology, Fii (Aquarius) is associated with leadership, water and happiness, inviting us to become a leader in our lives and to follow our own bliss, filling our cup from the waters of our own spiritual essence. Aquarius is ruled by the planet Uranus which is the planet of revolution and electricity. Uranus rules kundalini awakenings and everything that is connected to what is unique and different, and that is what this new moon is all about.

The moon will be conjunct Mercury which will be retrograde, so there is going to be an aspect of reflecting about the future. With two benefic planets Venus and Jupiter exactly conjunct at 12 degrees, we will feel full of love, harmony and happiness and we will realize that we do not have to strive, struggle or work hard to receive it. These two planets meeting together at the time of this new moon literally means that beautiful things will be attracted to us.

These energies will be enhanced by Brigid's presence here at Lunar Imbolg, who is connected with Venus and seeks to bring love and beauty into our lives. Ideally, this time should be spent out and about, engaging with as many people as possible. In this way, you will expose yourself to the greatest number of opportunities for growth and happiness. This conjunction also brings relationships of all kinds into focus and you may find yourself falling in love again.

WHERE IS THIS NEW MOON HAPPENING IN YOUR CHART?

SUN/RISING SIGN	ASTROLOGICAL HOUSE
Aries	11th house
Taurus	10th house
Gemini	9th house
Cancer	8th house
Leo	7th house
Virgo	6th house
Libra	5th house
Scorpio	4th house
Sagittarius	3rd house
Capricorn	2nd house
Aquarius	1st house
Pisces	12th house

Look to page 11 for the definition of each house.

NEW MOON
RITUAL

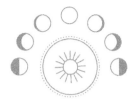

BRIGID'S CROSS MAKING

In this ritual, you're going to make a Brigid's cross / St. Bridget's cross. This is a traditional Imbolg practice from Ireland. The cross represents the four cardinal directions, the four sacred elements, the four seasons, and also represents the place where Spirit and Matter meet. It is said to bring protection to the home and is often hung on the front door. The cross is usually made with straw or rushes, which you will need for this ritual. There are many videos online giving demonstrations on how to make a Brigid's cross / St Bridget's cross. I have provided a YouTube link at the back of this book in the Additional Resources section.

Begin by opening sacred space (see page 21). Speak aloud any intentions that you have for connecting with Brigid. You may wish to ask for her support, protection, inspiration, or for healing. Your intention may also simply be to connect and get to know her.

Make your Brigid's cross / St. Bridget's cross. You may wish to play some Irish music as you do this. Once you've got the hang of the crafting of the cross, you can relax into a meditative state, focus on your intention, and open yourself up to feeling Brigid's energies.

Thank Brigid for hearing your intention and for her presence. Close sacred space (see page 23). Find a special place to hang your Brigid's cross / St. Bridget's cross where you will see it every day and be reminded of her.

FEBRUARY 27TH
FULL MOON IN VIRGO

12:18PM PST

PRIMARY INFLUENCE

Virgo (Classical) - Ech. (Celtic)

THEMES

All systems go!
Compassion
Practicality
Seeing the world through a higher
perspective

ASTROLOGY READING

We officially move forward on this full moon with all planets direct. This is significant because when all planets are direct it means that all systems go! Everything is moving forward, there are no planets moving backwards in the sky, and everyone is on the same page moving forwards.

This energy will be enhanced by the springtime energies that are beginning to grow between Imbolg and the Spring Equinox, also enhanced by the bountiful, fertile energies of Ech (Virgo). We have a couple of months of this which means it will be important for us to take advantage of this energy while it lasts. It has been months since we've gotten a chance to see all planets direct.

The sun has now officially entered into the sign of Pisces and invites us to dig deep into our compassionate heart and the invisible world that Ict (Pisces) naturally inhabits. With Venus also in the sign of Pisces this is a very dreamy time. The moon in Virgo is, however, at the opposite end of this spectrum. The moon in Virgo wants to make sure we are staying practical and looking at all of the details. The moon in Virgo can be perfectionistic, wanting us to make sure everything is in order.

The energy of this full moon will feel like we are observing everything going on from a distance. The moon is literally all alone in one part of the sky while all the other planets are huddled together on the other half of the sky.

We will have a higher perspective about everything going on, and we also might have feelings of being alone with our perspective, but this higher perspective will be the key to dealing with issues of healing our emotional wounds within ourselves and our communities. With Saturn, Jupiter and Mercury sextiling and trining the Nodes, this full moon is activating further progress in the world in terms of our collective destiny and the Aquarian Age.

WHERE IS THIS FULL MOON HAPPENING IN YOUR CHART?

SUN/RISING SIGN	ASTROLOGICAL HOUSE
Aries	6th house
Taurus	5th house
Gemini	4th house
Cancer	3rd house
Leo	2nd house
Virgo	1st house
Libra	12th house
Scorpio	11th house
Sagittarius	10th house
Capricorn	9th house
Aquarius	8th house
Pisces	7th house

Look to page 11 for the definition of each house.

FULL MOON RITUAL

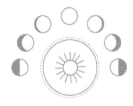

ANCHORING CORDS

This full moon, we have the polar opposite energies of the dreamy, celestial Pisces with the practical, grounded Virgo. In this simple ritual, you will practice anchoring into both the celestial realms and Mother Earth.

Close your eyes and deepen your breath. You may want to put on some music, light some candles and burn some herbs. See page 21 for guidance on opening sacred space.

Place one hand on your belly (the Warming Cauldron) and one hand on your mind space (the Cauldron of Knowledge). Feel an anchoring cord of light moving down from your belly, through your root and into Mother Earth, through the sands and soils, through rock and fire, to the very core of Mother Earth. As you deepen into this connection, you can say aloud, "I am opening and deepening into the Earth."

Once you have fully experienced this connection, you can turn your attention to the celestial realms. Feel an anchoring cord of light traveling up from your mind space, through cloud and rain, ether and plasma, through the golden codes of light from the sun, and anchoring into the cosmos. As you deepen into this connection, you can say aloud, "I am opening and expanding into the cosmos."

Once you've fully experienced this connection, you can give gratitude for Mother Earth and the celestial realms. Close sacred space (see page 23).

MARCH 13TH
NEW MOON IN PISCES

3:22AM PST

PRIMARY INFLUENCE

Pisces (Classical) - Ict. (Celtic)

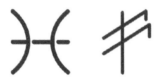

THEMES

Hopes, dreams and romantic desires
Self compassion
Psychic intuition
Empathy
Heightened sensitivities

ASTROLOGY READING

As we are finishing off the astrological year and getting ready for the Spring Equinox to arrive, we are going to experience this beautiful new moon in Pisces. The sun, the moon, Venus and Neptune will all be making a Pisces stellium in the sky.

This stellium will activate our hopes and dreams, our romantic desires, and our abilities to feel compassion for ourselves and others. This moon is pure healing space. It is about connecting to your heart, understanding others and feeling like we are all connected.

Pisces is the sign that rules the 12th house and the planet Neptune. This 12th house energy will be very apparent during this new moon. We will feel a deep connection to the divine, to everything that cannot be seen, the unknown territories of the subconscious mind, and the expansive universe along with the Akashic records. This is also mirrored in Celtic astrology with Ict (Pisces) being connected with the invisible realms.

Be ready to receive major downloads from the universe during this moon. I would highly recommend meditating and finding a practice that will help you tune into the frequencies of the divine essence of the universe. This moon is also about connecting to the higher dimensions, the crown chakra and the chakras outside the body that connect you to what exists beyond this 3-dimensional reality. With the sextile from the Moon to Pluto, all of our sensitivities will be heightened and the effect of this moon will be even stronger.

With Mars (who just moved into Gemini) trining Saturn in Aquarius, there will be an activation of deep passion, dedication and endurance that will help you to understand, communicate and express your ideas about what a new world can really look like. This moon feels very prophetic and we can be sure that with the Saturn square to Uranus, there will be some changes coming in the near future.

WHERE IS THIS NEW MOON HAPPENING IN YOUR CHART?

SUN/RISING SIGN	ASTROLOGICAL HOUSE
Aries	12th house
Taurus	11th house
Gemini	10th house
Cancer	9th house
Leo	8th house
Virgo	7th house
Libra	6th house
Scorpio	5th house
Sagittarius	4th house
Capricorn	3rd house
Aquarius	2nd house
Pisces	1st house

Look to page 11 for the definition of each house.

NEW MOON
RITUAL

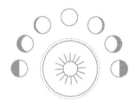

HEALING WATERS

In the Celtic tradition, water holds a lot of sacredness. There are wells around the Celtic lands where our ancestors would travel for healing and guidance. This is something that is still practiced today by those who follow the old ways. This full moon you are invited to participate in a simple water ritual that will help connect you to the healing, watery energies of Pisces.

Before you begin, you will need to gather some flowers. They can be harvested in the wild if they are available, or bought in a store, so long as they have petals. You will also need a bowl of water.

Begin by opening sacred space (see page 21). Take your bowl of water and your flowers and reflect on some things you would like to let go of in your life. Then reflect on some intentions that you'd like to set for the next moon cycle. Take one of the flower petals in your hands and focus on what you'd like to let go of. When you have this clear in your heart and mind, blow onto the petal. Then, turn the petal over and hold an intention for what you'd like to call in. Once you have this clear in your heart and mind, blow onto the petal. Place the petal into the water, and repeat with more petals until you feel complete.

Once you've finished, close sacred space (see page 23) and spend some time connecting with the moon and communing with her.

SPRING
EQUINOX

SPRING EQUINOX

Ostara/Eostre (Anglo Saxon) – Alban Eilir (Druid) – Easter (Christian)
Equal balance of light and darkness

SPRING EQUINOX PORTAL DATES

Spring Equinox: March 20th, 2021
Equinox portal: March 19th - March 21st

THEMES

Balance, new beginnings, fertility, rebirth,
integration of opposites, activation

SYMBOLS

Seeds, cosmic egg, hare, dragon,
bull, plough

HERBS, PLANTS & FLOWERS

Nettle, chickweed, apple leaf, snowdrop,
daisy, lemon balm

TRADITIONS

Planting seeds, painting eggs, flag making, baking hot
cross buns, spring cleaning

ARCHETYPES

The Maiden and the youthful Green Man

The Spring Equinox has been celebrated in the Celtic lands for at least 5000 years. Sacred sites such as Loughcrew (County Meath, Ireland) align with the position of the sun on Spring Equinox, where the ancient Celts would have gathered to welcome in the Spring.

I invite you to imagine life for the ancient Celts millennia ago. Imagine that in the long nights of winter, huddled together with your loved ones against the cold, you wondered, "Will we have enough food to last until Spring? Will our people survive? Will the light return?" And when Spring came, hope blossomed and we rejoiced in the rebirth of Mother Earth and the return of the sun. We celebrated the fertility and fecundity of the land and the turning of the great wheel of Life.

The Spring Equinox festival is a time of sacred balance and the union of polarities. It marks the first day of spring, the first planting of the crops, and a time of new beginnings. This is the time of the maiden and of initiation, when the energies of the earth are rebirthing and awakening. This is a time to shake off the cobwebs of winter, release what no longer serves us, and seed our dreams and longings into reality as we enter the active time of the year.

It's no coincidence that Ostara, Eostre, and Easter have similarities to the word estrogen and also East, which is the cardinal direction of springtime. This time of year is especially linked to feminine fertility, both physically and also metaphorically. This is a time for women to celebrate their seed centers (ovaries) and connect with the symbol of the cosmic egg which contains the sacred codes of creation; both light and darkness, masculine and feminine, conscious and unconscious.

There is an abundance of dragon energy at this time, representing the rising energies of the earth and the rising of energy in our bodies. The hare is revered for its connections to fertility and the unification of the inner and outer worlds, symbolized by the way the hare spends its life both above and below ground. At this time of year we also begin to see the emergence of the youthful aspect of the Green Man, who is the face in the trees and Lord of the Forest. Last but not least, the bull is revered at this time, who would help to plough the fields ready for planting, and whose head and horns look like the female reproductive system, connecting it to the sacred feminine.

HOT CROSS BUNS SPRING EQUINOX RECIPE

Bun ingredients:
- 4 earl grey tea bags
- 125g cranberries
- 150ml whole milk
- 50g butter
- 500g bread flour
- 1 tsp salt
- 75g sugar
- 7g easy yeast
- 1 egg
- 6 mandarins, zest
- ¾ tsp ground cardamom
- 1 tsp cinnamon
- ½ tsp allspice
- ¼ ground cloves
- ¼ tsp nutmeg

Cross ingredients:
- 40g flour
- 40g icing sugar
- 2 tsp mandarin juice
- 2 tbsp milk

Glaze ingredients:
- Apricot jam

BUN INSTRUCTIONS

Soak 125g cranberries in hot water for 1 hour.

Steep the earl grey tea bags in 160ml water for 15 minutes, then remove the tea bags.

Bring the milk to a boil and add the butter to melt. Add the earl grey tea. Make sure the liquid measures 300ml, otherwise top up with water. Allow to cool to 110°F (43°C).

Combine the flour, sugar, and yeast and mix together in a bowl.

Add the milk mixture, then beat an egg into the mixture. Add the salt. Continue mixing with a wooden spoon and then by hand (or do the whole process in a mixer).

Kneed for 5 minutes, until the mixture has a smooth, elastic texture.

Put into a lightly oiled bowl. Cover with oiled cling film, and make sure that it's tight to the surface of the dough. Allow to rise for 1 hour (until doubled in size).

Zest the mandarins and add to the dough. Drain the cranberries thoroughly, and add to the dough. Add in the spices. Begin mixing everything together with a wood spoon, and then with your hands.

Cover the mixture again with cling film, as before, and allow to rise until doubled in size (about 45 minutes).

Weigh the dough after the second rise and divide equally into 15 pieces.

Line 1-3 baking trays with parchment paper. Shape each piece into a ball, making sure the balls have a smooth surface on top. Use floured hands to shape them.

Place the buns on the baking trays, leaving enough room for each ball to double in size. Slash a cross into each bun with a sharp knife or lame.

Cover with a clean cloth kitchen towel and set aside to rise up to an hour.

CROSS AND GLAZE INSTRUCTIONS

Preheat the oven to 375°F (190°C).

Sieve the flour and icing sugar, and mix with the mandarin juice to make a paste. The consistency here is key more than the exact measurements. The consistency needs to be similar to the consistency of non-crystallized honey. It should run off the spoon in a steady, constant stream but without being too runny.

Transfer to a piping bag (you can use a plastic bag with a ½ inch / 1cm hole cut into the corner if you don't have a piping bag).

Brush the risen buns with milk, then pipe on the crosses.

Bake for 30 minutes until golden brown. Check them after 20 minutes and cover with aluminum foil if they begin to darken too much.

Gently heat the apricot jam to melt. Remove any large chunks or sieve it so there are no large chunks. You may want to add a splash of water to make the jam more runny, to spread more easily.

Lightly brush onto the warm buns and leave to cool.

Best eaten on the same day, but can keep for up to 5 days, and can also be frozen.

SPRING EQUINOX ASTROLOGY
MARCH 20TH

PRIMARY INFLUENCE

Aries (Classical) - Arb. (Celtic)

THEMES

The beginning
Springing into action
Empowered Feminine
Focusing on divine destiny
Connection to the mystical

ASTROLOGY READING

The Spring Equinox happens when the sun moves into the sign of Aries. This marks the beginning of the astrological new year in classical astrology. Aries is the beginning, it is life springing into action. Aries is like the Fool in the Tarot cards that believes he can achieve anything.

He moves forward with courage and not a single worry in the world. He is also naive and can be impulsive, but his energy is like a seed sprouting or a flower budding. There is a beautiful quote that describes this transition well by Anais Nin. The quote says "and the day came when the risk to remain tight in a bud was more painful than the risk it took to blossom".

Aries takes that risk wholeheartedly because it knows that on the other side is greatness. On the other side is life. On the other side is freedom. In Celtic astrology, Arb (Aires) is associated with the divine spark that ignites, activates and inspires. However, Arb is also associated with heritage, reminding us to ignite our inner flames with our roots deep in the soils of who we are and where we come from.

On this day, as the Sun enters the sign of Aries, it will conjunct the planet Chiron as well as Venus. Chiron is the planet of healing and Venus is the planet of love and relationships. What is really amazing is that just a few days after the Spring Equinox, Venus (the goddess of love and femininity) and the sun will make their superior conjunction. At the time of the Equinox, Venus will be disappearing from the morning sky view, into the rays of the Sun, ready to transform and integrate everything she has learned in the last 9 months.

Venus will soon re-emerge transformed and integrated as the Queen of Heaven and Earth. As she begins to re-emerge, she will now be seen in the evening sky, as the Evening Star. These powerful Venus-Sun cycles guide us closer towards our sacred divine feminine and it's remarkable that this conjunction is happening in alignment with the Spring Equinox!

Because this conjunction is happening in the sign of Aries, what we will begin to see in the world is the emergence of the strong warrior woman archetype, ready to take life head on, with courage, strength, independence and determination.

For the next 3 months we will also feel an intense awakening and desire to heal our deepest wounds and find compassion for ourselves and others. The moon and Mars will conjunct the North Node in Gemini on this day as well. This means that our emotional focus, our drive, and our desire to move towards our North Star, will all be aligned in the same energy of understanding life from a very real, down to earth perspective. The more we focus on what is right in front of us, the more we will discover the truth and know in what direction to move next.

Mercury will also be in the sign of Pisces on this day helping us tune our thoughts on infinite possibilities of healing, our intuition and a deep connection to the mystical.

MARCH 28th
FULL MOON IN LIBRA

11:48AM PST

PRIMARY INFLUENCE

Libra (Classical) - Ind. (Celtic)

THEMES

Balance and beauty
Venus rising
Activation of the higher mind
Communication
Healing portal

ASTROLOGY READING

This is the first full moon of the new year in Classical astrology, and it brings balance and beauty. In Celtic astrology, Libra represents the beginning of the astrological year and the 1st house, which weaves in beautifully with the new energies celebrated in Classical astrology on this day.

This Libra full moon will be in an aspect called a grand trine. The moon will trine Mars and the North Node and also trine Saturn. All these planets are in the element of air, making it a grand trine in air. This means that this moon will activate and intensify the intellectual mind in all of us. Saturn is going to play a big role in the unfolding of this full moon. He will be sextiling and trining both the full moon and the nodes, which means that the power of the moon is being channeled through the nodal axis, activating everything that has to do with leaving the karmic past behind and moving towards our true north, true purpose, and destiny.

With Mars conjunct the North Node on this day our drive will be to communicate, to talk, to listen, to express ourselves, and our ideas will be aligned with the collective destiny. Having the sun, Chiron and Venus all exactly conjunct at 8 degrees in Aries opposing the moon will create an interesting tension to the balance that the moon is seeking. Understanding that the number 8 is a sacred number, and the fact that it's appearing here in this chart multiple times (Uranus, moon, sun, Chiron and Venus all at 8 degrees) means that this moon has a sacred message to bring us. It's a portal that's opening up to allow true healing to happen in our relationships.

The sacred divine feminine is awakening in her power. This Venus-Sun portal began with the Spring Equinox. In terms of the sacred feminine awakening powerfully in the collective, many people may not understand it because Venus is the goddess of love, but in Aries she can be a bit selfish and impulsive. The same goes with the sun in Aries. It feels free to do what it wants without thinking about the consequences or how it is going to make anyone else feel. However, with Chiron sandwiched between these two planets, there will be a healing connection created that will release the need for everything to be about us, and to understand that a new wave of the feminine is rising.

Venus also rules this Libra moon, and she is challenging the normal view of what the feminine represents. The moon is pointing the way towards balance while Venus is emerging with new power.

WHERE IS THIS FULL MOON HAPPENING IN YOUR CHART?

SUN/RISING SIGN	ASTROLOGICAL HOUSE
Aries	7th house
Taurus	6th house
Gemini	5th house
Cancer	4th house
Leo	3rd house
Virgo	2nd house
Libra	1st house

SUN/RISING SIGN CONTINUED	ASTROLOGICAL HOUSE CONTINUED

Scorpio	12th house
Sagittarius	11th house
Capricorn	10th house
Aquarius	9th house
Pisces	8th house

Look to page 11 for the definition of each house.

FULL MOON
RITUAL

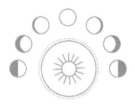

NATURE WALK

In the Celtic isles this is the time of "the quickening", when the natural world begins to blossom, grow and transform with great speed. "The quickening" is similar to the time during pregnancy when the baby begins to grow very rapidly, a time when new life is rising from the depths.

This full moon you are invited to take a walk in nature to take in the sights and smells and sounds of the budding spring. Make this a sacred experience by walking with presence as if each step is kissing the earth. Look around with a soft gaze, really observing all that's around you. Veer off the path, touch the earth, be with the trees and the springtime flowers.

APRIL 11TH
NEW MOON IN ARIES

7:31AM PST

PRIMARY INFLUENCE

Aires (Classical) - Arb. (Celtic)

THEMES

Manifestation
Excitement
Power struggles in relationships
Initiation

ASTROLOGY READING

This Aries new moon will have a lot of planets backing it up. There will be an Aries stellium in the sky with the moon, sun, Mercury, Chiron, and Venus. This fiery new moon will be a great opportunity to set your intentions for the Spring and ask yourself, what do I want to manifest in my life?

What seeds do I want to sprout in the next few months? Aries lends itself to powerful activation energy, that when used wisely, can help you take action towards what you want. Similarly in Celtic astrology, Arb (Aires) is represented by the fiery ram and helps to spark things into motion. This is a day where we will feel excited, ready to take action, and driven towards asserting ourselves.

With Venus in an exact square to Pluto, this will bring up intense attraction in relationships, but it can also cause power struggles in our relationships. Aries is a very independent energy and Capricorn is a grounded and responsible energy. We may feel as if we are not being seen or heard or taken seriously, or we may feel like others are not being responsible right now. Either way, this moon can help you initiate great things in your life.

WHERE IS THIS NEW MOON HAPPENING IN YOUR CHART?

SUN/RISING SIGN	ASTROLOGICAL HOUSE
Aries	1st house
Taurus	12th house
Gemini	11th house
Cancer	10th house
Leo	9th house
Virgo	8th house
Libra	7th house
Scorpio	6th house
Sagittarius	5th house
Capricorn	4th house
Aquarius	3rd house
Pisces	2nd house

Look to page 11 for the definition of each house.

NEW MOON
RITUAL

BURLÁ GHUÍ

In this ritual you are going to make Burlá Ghuí (pronounced bur-la gwee), which means a prayer bundle in Irish. The prayers are made in the form of nature items to represent whatever the intention is for and placed into the bundle. At the end of the ritual, you will either bury or burn the bundle, releasing your intentions to a greater power.

For this ritual you will need a biodegradable cloth or piece of paper (such as cheesecloth or tissue paper) as well as biodegradable string (such as twine). You will also need a variety of nature items to place into the bundle such as seeds, berries, leaves, flowers, ashes, honey.

Begin by opening sacred space (see page 21). Set your cloth or paper in front of you, and the natural items around the edges ready to be placed into the bundle. Put on music that speaks to your soul. Take a handful of natural items into your hands. As you're holding the items, focus on either an intention of something you want to call into your life, or something that you're ready to let go of. Once you have this clear in your mind, speak it aloud and scatter the items into the bundle. Do this slowly, with presence, as if making a beautiful piece of art. Repeat this process until you feel complete with all of your intentions and all that you're letting go of.

Fold your piece of cloth or paper into a bundle and tie it with your string. Close sacred space (see page 23).

APRIL 26TH, LUNAR BEALTAINE
FULL MOON IN SCORPIO

8:31PM PST

PRIMARY INFLUENCE

Scorpio (Classical) - Lii. (Celtic)

THEMES

Deep intuition
Discomfort
Beyond the veil
A call to grounding

ASTROLOGY READING

The moon in Scorpio is in its fall position. Although Scorpio is a very deep, intuitive sign, and a water sign which is also the realm of the moon, the moon in its fall position is at its worst, its lowest point, where it doesn't want to be doing what it is being asked to do.

The moon prefers to be in the sign of Taurus, where it is exalted, or Cancer, where it's dignified. But in Scorpio, it's asked to go into the realm of Pluto, of intensity, drama, jealousy and revenge. In Celtic astrology, Lii (Scorpio) is connected with the house of arriving and coming to place, and is symbolized by the compass. With this full moon it's going to feel a bit like wandering through the immortal dream spaces but without a compass and without any sense of arriving anywhere.

To add to this energy, we have a stellium in Taurus opposing the moon. The sun, Uranus, Venus and Mercury are together in Taurus asking us to try to see the beauty in everything and to find as much grounding as we possibly can. Taurus is the sign of the Bull and the Earth Goddess. She desires to be comfortable amongst a flush green forest, or grounded within a vibrant jungle full of life. She desires to be connected to the Earth and everything that is of value. In Celtic astrology, Insci (Taurus) is represented by the symbol of the heart or udder, which also speaks to these grounded, earthly, feminine energies. This moon is asking us not to be afraid to see beyond the veil, or of change and transformation. Additionally, Saturn will be T-squaring the full moon creating some tension to be resolved. The tension will be between our deepest desires and what we truly value in life.

WHERE IS THIS FULL MOON HAPPENING IN YOUR CHART?

SUN/RISING SIGN	ASTROLOGICAL HOUSE
Aries	8th house
Taurus	7th house
Gemini	6th house
Cancer	5th house
Leo	4th house
Virgo	3rd house
Libra	2nd house
Scorpio	1st house
Sagittarius	12th house
Capricorn	11th house
Aquarius	10th house
Pisces	9th house

Look to page 11 for the definition of each house.

FULL MOON
RITUAL

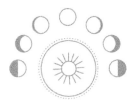

FLOWER MANDALA

There are so many beautiful flowers abundant at this time of year in the Celtic lands and beyond. The invitation for this ritual is to harvest some wildflowers and create a beautiful mandala out in nature with deep prayer and intention. You can also use store bought flowers if wildflowers are not available. You will also have the opportunity to do a symbolic 'jump over the fire' in honor of Lunar Bealtaine using a candle (you can read more about this tradition in the following pages).

Go to a special place in nature (if possible, otherwise indoors) with your flowers and candle. Open sacred space (see page 21). Create a flower mandala using the petals from your flowers, focusing your attention on what you're ready to let go of and what you're ready to call into your life. Once the flower mandala is finished, light your candle and jump over the candle, symbolizing your leap of faith as you let go of the old and welcome in the new.

You may also want to leave a special offering to the Horned God and the May Queen in your special place in nature, along with Mother Earth, Father Sky, and the Ancestors. These offerings should be something meaningful to you, to give the offering extra potency. Complete the ritual by closing sacred space (see page 23).

BEALTAINE

BEALTAINE

Bealtaine/Beltane (Celtic)
Midway point between Spring Equinox and Summer Solstice

BEALTAINE PORTAL KEY DATES

Lunar Bealtaine: April 26th, 2021 (8:31pm PST)
Traditional celebration date: May 1st
Solar Bealtaine: May 5th, 2021 (12:00am Pacific)

THEMES

Sacred union, sexual expression, purification,
protection, fertility, transformation

SYMBOLS

Tree of life, flower crowns and garlands, morning
dew, red and white ribbons, union of the divine
masculine and divine feminine, faeries (na Sídhe)

HERBS, PLANTS & FLOWERS

Hawthorne, apple blossom, rose, bluebell, ivy, honeysuckle,
marigold, lilac, violet, tulips, kingcups, meadow-orchids

TRADITIONS

Maypole, dancing, handfastings, purification rituals,
jumping over the fire

ARCHETYPES

The May Queen & Green Man as the Lovers

Bealtaine marks the height of springtime and transition into early summer,
and is celebrated at the halfway point between the Spring Equinox and
the Summer Solstice. Bealtaine is a fire festival, and is traditionally
celebrated on May 1st, but due to the change in the earth's axis of rotation
over time this point is now closer to May 5th. Some observe May 5th as
"Old Beltane," however the traditional date of May 1st is usually still
favored.

In Celtic communities, the fire in people's homes would have been
extinguished, and a great fire was lit - the Neid fire - which would have
been used for different kinds of purification and protection ceremonies at
this time, both for people and animals alike. After the fire burned for three
days, the embers of the great fire would have been used to relight the
fires in peoples' homes.

Bealtaine is a time of sacred union between the divine feminine and the divine masculine, which gives birth to new life. This is a time to celebrate nature's renewal and the growing season which brings abundance. On Bealtaine many couples would be handfasted, which is an ancient custom that's similar to marriage but was often only for a year and day, after which they could choose to renew their vows or not.

Once handfasted, couples jumped over the great fire to purify themselves of their old lives and welcome in their new life as a wedded couple. Flowers were an important part of the Bealtaine celebrations, representing the blossoming summertime, fertility and sexuality, with the opening petals representing female sexuality. Flowers are also very much associated with the Faery realm. Maidens would wear flower crowns and place flowers around their communities for luck and protection.

Bealtaine stands across the wheel of the year from Samhain and, like Samhain, is a time when the veil between the worlds is very thin, when Spirits walk among us, and we are able to go between the world of Spirit (the Otherworld) and the world of Matter. The Sidhe (faeries) are also active during the Bealtaine portal, who would have been both feared and revered for bringing both magic and mischief.

STRAWBERRY PUNCH
BEALTAINE RECIPE

Ingredients:

- 8 cups of water, divided (1840ml)
- 1 cup of granulated sugar
- 1 ½ pints of fresh strawberries, hulled
- 2 cups freshly squeezed lemon juice (approximately 8 lemons)
- Mint sprigs, for garnish

Combine 2 cups of water (460ml), the sugar and the strawberries in a blender or food processor. Process until the mixture is smooth.

Transfer to a pitcher and add the remaining 6 cups of water (1380ml) and the lemon juice. Stir well until combined.

Serve with a sprig of mint over ice.

In England, the strawberry is sometimes referred to as "queen of berries." The strawberry season officially starts on May 1st and finishes at the end of September.

BEALTAINE ASTROLOGY
MAY 1st

PRIMARY INFLUENCE

Taurus (Classical) - Insci. (Celtic)

THEMES

The earth goddess
Soul activation
Unpredictability
Activation of the divine feminine

ASTROLOGY READING

The energy of Taurus is very strong on this day. We will see the sun, Uranus, Venus and Mercury in a Taurus stellium in the sky. The most powerful significance of this astrological alignment is the fact that the sun is conjunct Uranus, which is an activation of our Soul.

This can manifest as a desire to express our unique qualities, to be innovative, to set ourselves free, and to revolt against anything that tries to restrict our freedom. Sun conjunct Uranus is also a revolution of the collective Soul of humanity. Uranus in Taurus is about building a new world and the sun in Taurus is about finding comfort in your material world. These two planets are asking us to be okay with change, unpredictability, and the kundalini fire rising through our bodies.

On this day, in which we celebrate the union of the divine masculine and divine feminine, we also see the energies of the lovers in the sky. Taurus is represented by the bull as the Horned God in the sky. However, Taurus is also ruled by Venus, representing the powerful activation of the divine feminine, the May Queen in the sky. These two energies together in sacred marriage create a powerful portal of transformation. Venus in Taurus will urge you to find the things that bring you pleasure in life; to connect to Mother Earth, to walk barefoot, connect with the elements, and to feel the fertile nature of the land. This is the way of the Horned God and the May Queen. Mercury, the planet of the mind, also in Taurus, will help align our thoughts to all of this energy that is coming forward.

In essence, all of these planets are asking us to fully be in our sacred divine feminine and to allow the kundalini energy that rises from the earth up towards the sky to be fully activated in passion, desire, unpredictability and pleasure.

In Celtic astrology, Insci (Taurus) is ruled by Riia (Venus) just as in Classical astrology, and is represented by the symbol of the heart, reminding us to stay true to our heartfelt longings and desires. Insci is also connected with the house of speech and discourse, reminding us to express what lives in our hearts with truth and sincerity.

MAY 11TH,
NEW MOON IN TAURUS

12PM PST

PRIMARY INFLUENCE

Taurus (Classical) - Insci. (Celtic)

THEMES

Auspicious energies
Comfort and pleasure
Unpredictability
Vulnerability
Preparation for eclipse season

ASTROLOGY READING

The powerful thing about a new moon in Taurus is that the moon is exalted in this sign. When a planet is in exaltation it feels really comfortable, like it's on vacation. A planet in exaltation is in its second favorite sign. So the moon feels good here, and Taurus is all about financial gain, stability, grounding, the goddess, fertility and values.

These are the themes that are coming up with this moon. There is going to a Taurus stellium in the sky as well as a Gemini stellium. The most remarkable thing about this Taurus stellium is that Uranus (the planet of revolution, electricity and innovation) is part of this stellium. Uranus in Taurus has been teaching us how to build a new world. This means that there are many unpredictable events that are emerging from this new moon.

When Uranus comes together with the sun it creates an independent, free spirited energy that wants to show off its uniqueness. It's spontaneous and willing to go along with change if necessary. When Uranus comes together with the moon, our emotions can become unpredictable. But the power of this Taurus new moon is that it's asking us to get innovative and bring abundance, creativity, and manifestation back into our lives.

With Mars squaring Chiron, our vulnerability becomes our strength and with the sextile to Uranus from Mars, we will feel a burst of incredible energy and a desire for adventure!

The Yod that Mars and Uranus are making to the South Node are giving us a clue about how to heal old karmic wounds, old past traumas, and how to let go of belief systems that no longer serve us. With Jupiter at the last degrees of Aquarius, Uranus has a big surge of power, since it rules the sign of Aquarius. The last degrees of any sign creates an intense energy where that planet wants to fully actualize itself before it moves into the next zodiac sign.

Jupiter has been expanding our focus on humanity, on the Aquarian Age, on community, groups, and the future. With the trine to Pluto from the moon we will feel very internally connected to the truth. This new moon is the last moon before we enter into eclipse season again, so the energy is beginning to build up.

With Venus and Mercury conjunct the North Node we are being asked to focus on the future of our relationships, on communicating within all of our relationships, and on continuing to move forward collectively towards a better understanding amongst each other. These themes are enhanced by the energies of Insci (Taurus) in Celtic astrology which are associated with speech, discourse, sincerity and truth.

WHERE IS THIS NEW MOON HAPPENING IN YOUR CHART?

SUN/RISING SIGN	ASTROLOGICAL HOUSE
Aries	2nd house
Taurus	1st house
Gemini	12th house

SUN/RISING SIGN (CONTINUED)	ASTROLOGICAL HOUSE (CONTINUED)
Cancer	11th house
Leo	10th house
Virgo	9th house
Libra	8th house
Scorpio	7th house
Sagittarius	6th house
Capricorn	5th house
Aquarius	4th house
Pisces	3rd house

Look to page 11 for the definition of each house.

NEW MOON
RITUAL

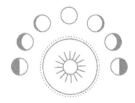

CLOOTIE RITUAL

In the Celtic tradition, people would use "clooties" for intention setting and prayers. If you go to a sacred well in the Celtic isles, you will often find a nearby tree filled with them, which are usually strips of cloth tied to the branches. This knot magic serves as a way of focusing an intention in the physical realm, and is often used as a prayer for healing of some kind.

In this ritual the invitation is to find a tree that feels special to you. Bring a ribbon or piece of cloth with you, set your intention and tie the cloth to the tree, keeping the intention clear in your heart and mind as you tie the knot. Make sure the fabric is biodegradable so that it will disintegrate over time in the elements.

MAY 26TH - FULL MOON LUNAR ECLIPSE IN SAGITTARIUS

4:14AM PST

PRIMARY INFLUENCE

Sagittarius (Classical) - Rii. (Celtic)

THEMES

The next 6 months
Change and transformation
Adventure
Compassion and generosity
Healing the karmic past

ASTROLOGY READING

We arrive once again at eclipse season, where the world is asked to transform powerfully again. This eclipse season is closing off the last six months and opening up a portal to jump forward into the next 6 months. The moon in Sagittarius will square Jupiter, trine Chiron and conjunct the South Node.

Sagittarius is adventurous by nature, reflected in Celtic astrology with Rii (Sagittarius) who is symbolized by the horse, representing travel. But the adventurous spirit of this Sagittarius moon is dampened a bit when it conjuncts the South Node in Sagittarius. The lessons of South Node in Sagittarius are about not believing everything we hear, about letting go of belief systems that are false, and about moving towards a more factual understanding of reality based on what we see in front of us right here, right now.

Jupiter in Aquarius has taught us all about a new philosophy of life. Now in Pisces, it will open us up to compassion and generosity, and we will desire to be of help to others. Jupiter is going to expand our emotions at this time and no one will have to guess how we feel because it will be obvious. Everything is easily seen on the surface, expressed in a very outward way.

Moon trine Chiron creates an opportunity for a powerful balance of emotions and the higher self in consciousness. This is about creating more harmony in our lives. Chiron calms the moon down with its healing powers.

This moon is a moment for us to reconnect with our strategy for winning the game, being successful, and moving forward towards a better future. Saturn has also recently gone retrograde and we must now reflect on the time between December 21st 2020 and now. What can we do differently? What worked and what didn't? These are the questions to reflect on right now, especially as we begin to approach the Summer Solstice, when we will shift from the waxing half of the year (ruled by the Oak King) to the waning half of the year (ruled by the Holly King).

WHERE IS THIS FULL MOON HAPPENING IN YOUR CHART?

SUN/RISING SIGN	ASTROLOGICAL HOUSE
Aries	9th house
Taurus	8th house
Gemini	7th house
Cancer	6th house
Leo	5th house
Virgo	4th house
Libra	3rd house
Scorpio	2nd house
Sagittarius	1st house
Capricorn	12th house
Aquarius	11th house
Pisces	10th house

Look to page 11 for the definition of each house.

FULL MOON
RITUAL

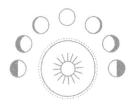

HONORING THE FAE

This is an invitation to do a ritual outside in nature to honor the fae and the elementals and set an intention to connect with them. It's best to do this in a place that feels sacred to you in some way, such as a nemeton (a meadow surrounded by forest), stone circle, mound or hill, or at the water's edge.

At the beginning of the ritual, it's important to call for protection. Some people like to imagine an energetic bubble of protection around them. You may want to call on a guide that you have a relationship with who has your best intentions at heart. Part of this protection is also staying grounded and in the present moment. Feel the presence of Mother Earth beneath you, and approach the ritual from your heart space instead of your mind space.

You are then invited to leave some kind of offering to honor the fae/elementals. You do not need to make direct contact with these spirits, you are invited to simply honor them, and know that you are being witnessed. Traditional faery offerings include honey, oats or flowers, or all three. With your physical offering, you may want to offer some kind of prayer or intention for humankind to come back into balance with nature.

Once you've left your offerings, thank the spirits who came to witness you, even if you don't sense or see them. Really pay attention to any shifts of energies, any visions that come to mind, and any feelings or sensations.

JUNE 10TH – NEW MOON
SOLAR ECLIPSE IN GEMINI

3:53AM PST

PRIMARY INFLUENCE

Gemini (Classical) - Ruidzuig (Celtic)

THEMES

Deep revolutionary reflection
Communication
Determination
Awareness

ASTROLOGY READING

As we move into the second eclipse of the season, Mercury has now gone retrograde in Gemini, its ruling sign. This retrograde will be felt more than others because Mercury is conjunct the moon, sun and North Node. Mercury retrograde can affect communication, travel, transportation, and technology.

There will also be an opposition from Mars to Pluto that will activate our desire to never give up on our goals. Pluto brings in an intensity that is unheard of from any other planet. The Mercury conjunction to the moon will make us a lot more aware of our feelings and we will have to reflect on whether we have communicated what we wanted and how we wanted.

The intention that this eclipse is setting for us for the next 6 months is about remembering this: without seeing the truth right in front of you, it's difficult to know where you're headed in life. In Celtic astrology, Ruidzuig (Gemini) is connected with the cosmic egg and death, inviting us to shed our egoic self to liberate our higher consciousness in a radical rebirthing process, which feels potent during this eclipse.

The moon will also be trining Saturn, which will help us be more practical and realistic during this time. What we need to be careful of during this time is to not get lost in our illusions and fantasies. The square to Neptune will challenge us to face reality.

WHERE IS THIS NEW MOON HAPPENING IN YOUR CHART?

SUN/RISING SIGN	ASTROLOGICAL HOUSE
Aries	3rd house
Taurus	2nd house
Gemini	1st house
Cancer	12th house
Leo	11th house
Virgo	10th house
Libra	9th house
Scorpio	8th house
Sagittarius	7th house
Capricorn	6th house
Aquarius	5th house
Pisces	4th house

Look to page 11 for the definition of each house.

NEW MOON
RITUAL

JOURNALING PRACTICE

For this powerful new moon eclipse, you are invited to spend some time reflecting and simply being, to take in these powerful energies. Here are a few journaling questions for you to explore:

What dreams are you willing to fight for, no matter how difficult they are to achieve?

What are some practical next steps you need to take to make these dreams a reality?

What blessing is this new moon energy amplifying in your life?

SUMMER
SOLSTICE

SUMMER SOLSTICE

Midsummer - Litha (Anglo-Saxon) - Alban Hefin (Druid) - St John's Day
Christian) - The longest day and shortest night of the year

SUMMER SOLSTICE PORTAL DATES

Summer Solstice: June 20th, 2021
Solstice portal: June 19th - June 21st

THEMES

Light codes, universal golden truths, duality,
realization, manifestation, vitality

SYMBOLS

Divine masculine and feminine, light and darkness,
fire and water, tree of life, Oak King & Holly King,
circle of life, wheel of fire, Celtic cross

HERBS, PLANTS & FLOWERS

St. John's Wort, chamomile, calendula, lavender, meadowsweet,
verbena, sage, mint, elder and roses

TRADITIONS

Neid fire, candlelight processions, fire magic, visiting
sacred wells for healing, collecting herbs and
wildcrafting

ARCHETYPES

The Divine Mother & Divine Father

Summer Solstice is the longest day and shortest night of the year, with Winter Solstice on the opposite side of the wheel. Both of these solstice events are celebrated over three days, when the sun appears to stand still in the sky (in Irish, the Solstice is called 'Grianstad' which literally means 'sun stop'). This festival has been celebrated for thousands of years, and is still celebrated today on the Celtic isles and beyond. Midsummer's Eve was just as important as Midsummer's day. People would perform candlelight processions and stay up through the night to welcome in the sunrise.

Above all, this festival is a celebration of light. It's a time of heightened energy, full expression, realization and manifestation.

This is a time to connect with the light beings, the ascended masters, and the golden universal truths. This is a time when the Great Sun and Mother Earth, the divine father and divine mother, are in their full expression. This is a time to connect with solar light codes and the energies of ascension, and to remember who we are and where we come from. This is also very much a time of fertility and abundance.

With the union of the divine masculine and divine feminine at Bealtaine, the Great Mother is now pregnant with life. With all of the sexual activity and handfastings at Bealtaine, many of the womenfolk would also be pregnant. The fields that were planted at Bealtaine are growing fast now, and more seeds are being planted.

We also bring awareness to the fact that what rises, falls. What comes, goes. This is a reminder of the impermanence of life, as the days will become shorter after this day. The outer energy begins to contract, and the inner energy begins to expand. Therefore, there is a dual nature to this celebration. It is both a celebration of the light and a celebration of the return to darkness, honoring the wheel of Life and the balance of all things. This is the time when the Oak King (who is the ruler of the waxing half of the year, when the days grow longer) is crowned and then dies so that the Holly King can be reborn (who is the ruler of the waning half of the year, when the days grow shorter).

ROSEWATER, GINGER, CARDAMOM COOKIES SUMMER SOLSTICE RECIPE

Cookie ingridients:
- 1 cup brown rice flour
- 2 cups flaxseed meal
- 1 tbsp cardamom
- 1 tbsp ground ginger
- 2 tbsp rosewater
- 2 tbsp olive oil
- 1 tbsp vanilla extract
- 1 tbsp baking powder
- 1 cup maple syrup
- 1 egg
- 2 pinches salt

For the garnish:
- Pistachios
- Dried rose petals

Mix all the cookie ingredients together in a large bowl. Kneed into small, tightly packed balls, and make a small indentation in the top of each cookie. Add a garnish of pistachio and dried rose petals.

Preheat the oven to 375°F (180°C)
Bake for 15-20 minutes.
Take out of the oven and let cool.

SUMMER SOLSTICE ASTROLOGY
JUNE 20TH

PRIMARY INFLUENCE

Cancer (Classical) - Iul. (Celtic)

THEMES

Passion, desire and manifestation
Heart chakra activation
Spiritual and philosophical growth
The mother

ASTROLOGY READING

As the Sun moves into the sign of Cancer and has reached its ultimate power, we will see a grand trine of fire in the sky. This grand trine of fire will include Mars in Leo (our drive to be seen and valued), Chiron in Aries (our desire to heal), and the South Node in Sagittarius (our need to leave behind all that has passed and no longer serves us).

Grand trines in fire activate our passion and desire to manifest and create things. During the Summer Solstice we experience the growth of all the seeds we planted in the Spring literally and metaphorically, and by this point in the Sun's zodiacal journey we have reached our heart center.

The sign of Cancer is ruled by the Moon which brings our focus to our emotions and the divine feminine, which is probably why the archetype of the Mother is used to describe this phase of the Sun's journey. Cancer asks us to drop from our heads to our heart, to use our intuition, and to listen deeply to the calling of our Soul.

The union of fire and water influences in the sky are in perfect harmony with the energies of Summer Solstice, especially with the fiery sun (representing the Divine Father) moving into watery Cancer (representing the Divine Mother). In Celtic astrology, Iul (Cancer) is ruled by Gaelach (Moon), as in Classical astrology, and is associated with honesty and will. This day asks us to be honest with ourselves and to align our will with the will of the Divine Mother and Father.

The watery celestial energies at this time will be enhanced by the fact that Jupiter will go retrograde on this day in the sign of Pisces. Because Jupiter is the planet of expansion and our highest spiritual awakening, his retrograde begins a process of intense spiritual and philosophical growth. This is a period to reconnect with your inner compass, inner truth and higher consciousness.

With Jupiter in Pisces, we are called to understand our connection to the divine and the mystical that lives within each and every one of us. On this day we will also see the sun and Jupiter begin to get closer to their exact trine on June 23rd. Sun trine Jupiter brings good luck, expansion of the Soul, and prosperity into everything we do.

JUNE 24TH
FULL MOON IN CAPRICORN

11:39AM PST

PRIMARY INFLUENCE

Capricorn (Classical) - Lu. (Celtic)

♑ ᚠ

THEMES

Auspicious energy
Prosperity and good luck
Setting long term goals
Control of the emotions

ASTROLOGY READING

This full moon is a very auspicious one. The day before this moon, the Sun and Jupiter finally make their exact trine to each other at 2 degrees. Sun-Jupiter days are days of good luck, beginning new business projects and planting the seeds for anything that you want to grow fast in your life.

Some people get married on Sun-Jupiter days to bring in the most luck to their marriage. Some people launch businesses or projects on this type of day. It's a good day to mark in your calendar because of its potent power, bringing good luck to whatever you begin. In Celtic astrology, Lu (Capricorn) is associated with abundance and wealth, enhancing the energies of good fortune in the material realm.

The day after this exact Sun-Jupiter trine, the moon reaches its full phase. Although the sun and Jupiter are not exactly conjunct at 2 degrees anymore, but are 1 degree apart, they are still in a trine (within the allowed orb) and so this full moon gives this trine more power. The moon in Capricorn, although in its detriment, is about being practical, setting long-term goals and putting in the work needed to reach those goals. Capricorn is the sign of success and business and although this is a foreign playing field for the moon, she will help us to control our emotions.

We have to remember also that Jupiter has just gone retrograde, so it's not at its full power but in the sign of Pisces. This is a powerful time to reflect on how much you've grown and expanded while Jupiter was direct.

WHERE IS THIS FULL MOON HAPPENING IN YOUR CHART?

SUN/RISING SIGN	ASTROLOGICAL HOUSE
Aries	10th house
Taurus	9th house
Gemini	8th house
Cancer	7th house
Leo	6th house
Virgo	5th house
Libra	4th house
Scorpio	3rd house
Sagittarius	2nd house
Capricorn	1st house
Aquarius	12th house
Pisces	11th house

Look to page 11 for the definition of each house.

FULL MOON
RITUAL

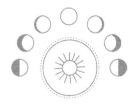

SOLAR INFUSION

Infusing water with solar energies creates a beautiful solar infusion for ritual work. You can use the elixir for anointing, land offerings, and ritual baths.

Fill a jar with a variety of herbs and plants that you want to make your infusion with. Some ideas include dandelion, lemon balm, peppermint, and raspberry leaf*. All of these herbs together make a really nice tea. Add roughly ½ cup (6 tbsp) of herbs per quart. You can use tea bags or put the herbs in a muslin bag or cheesecloth for ease.

A general time frame is between 2-3 hours of sunshine, but if it's a really hot day you may want to bring it in after 1 hour. Be very careful with how long you leave it out for as bacteria can grow.

Once the sun tea is the color and flavor you're going for, take the herbs out and you can sweeten the tea with agave or honey. Drink the tea right away or put it in the fridge and drink within a few days.

*Make sure to do your own research when ingesting herbs, especially if you're on any kind of medication.

JULY 9TH
NEW MOON IN CANCER

6:17 PM PST

PRIMARY INFLUENCE

Cancer (Classical) - Iul. (Celtic)

THEMES

Tension is in the air
Focusing on the heart center
Intense emotions
Humbling energies

ASTROLOGY READING

Since the last full moon the energy has been a bit intense. We have seen Neptune go retrograde, Venus enter the sign of Leo, Mars oppose Saturn and square Uranus, the sun square Chiron and Venus oppose Saturn and square Uranus.

When we see a lot of oppositions and squares we know that tension is in the air. Squares and oppositions create situations that need to be resolved and this new moon in cancer is an opportunity to resolve this tension. Mars opposed Saturn is about feeling like there are obstacles in the way of achieving the things you want to do.

With Mars square Uranus however, we have the desire to change things. The Venus aspects create tension in our relationships similar to Mars, and we end up wanting to make changes. When we arrive at this new moon in Cancer, we are able to bring the focus back to home, back to our heart center and ask ourselves, what is it that we want in life? What feels like home to us? With Iul (Cancer) representing honesty and will in Celtic astrology, this is a good time to be really honest with yourself and harness the power of your free will.

This moon will be opposing Pluto which will intensify our emotions. We will feel a push and pull between allowing our emotions to flow freely and restricting them, creating an emotional power struggle within ourselves. A square to Chiron from the moon will create a crisis over our feelings and higher consciousness. To rise out of the crisis we have to gain a higher perspective on everything going on.

Venus will be conjunct Mars in the sign of Leo making a grand trine in fire to the South Node and Chiron, activating our passion and desire to be the best, to shine brightly in our relationships, to understand that we have both feminine and masculine aspects within us and to find balance within. With Mars and Venus conjunct in Leo, we want to be seen and take action towards being seen. In Celtic astrology, Og (Leo) wants to shine brightly, but it's also associated with humility. It's important that we feel valued at this time, while also staying humble. The trine to Neptune from the moon will help us approach this gently and with compassion.

WHERE IS THIS NEW MOON HAPPENING IN YOUR CHART?

SUN/RISING SIGN	ASTROLOGICAL HOUSE
Aries	4th house
Taurus	3rd house
Gemini	2nd house
Cancer	1st house
Leo	12th house
Virgo	11th house
Libra	10th house
Scorpio	9th house
Sagittarius	8th house
Capricorn	7th house
Aquarius	6th house
Pisces	5th house

Look to page 11 for the definition of each house.

NEW MOON
RITUAL

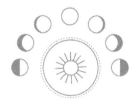

JOURNALING PRACTICE

This new moon, take some time to be really honest with yourself. There are a lot of tensions happening with this moon. Here are a few journal questions for you to reflect on.

What do you truly want at this moment in your life?

What does "home" mean to you?

With all that you're creating at this active time of year, how can you nurture yourself more fully?

JULY 23TH
FULL MOON IN AQUARIUS

7:37PM PST

PRIMARY INFLUENCE

Aquarius (Classical) - Fii. (Celtic)

THEMES

Deep inner reflection
An internal process
Possible emotional volatility
Dealing with our shadow side

ASTROLOGY READING

Jupiter, Saturn, Chiron, Neptune and Pluto are now all retrograde and we are feeling the deep reflective nature of these retrogrades. These times feel heavy because they are about working internally with ourselves.

This full moon might feel a bit volatile because the moon is conjunct Pluto which tends to create intensity and drama. On the opposite side of the chart we have the sun who just entered into the sign of Leo. The sun rules the sign of Leo, so it feels at its utmost power. However, the opposition to Pluto creates a massive internal struggle to express itself. If the sun represents the Soul and our Soul needs to be able to shine brightly, Pluto dims that light and creates a shadow that is difficult to get out from under. This is symbolic of a battle between the Ego and the Soul, or heaven and hell, or God and the Devil. It's the dark forces of Pluto causing our emotions to go out of control, making us feel like we are not in control of ourselves at all.

It will be important for us on this day to remember that we are here to fulfill a starseed mission and we must not give into an outside force that only seeks control of the people, which is what Aquarius represents. Many of us might feel like escaping or running away from the energies and some of us will feel very rebellious. In Celtic astrology, Fii (Aquarius) is associated with leadership as a pathway to happiness, bliss, and spiritual fulfillment. This is a good time to connect with these energies and remind yourself to take control of your life, and not to give your power away to anyone.

Jupiter is also about to retrograde back into the sign of Aquarius where it will give the people, the communities, the collective their power back. Another thing to point out is that the Nodes have finally entered their last decan in Gemini and Sagittarius. In about 6 months they will be switching to the signs of Taurus and Scorpio, which will completely change the collective energy and focus of the future of humanity. Lastly, this full moon in Aquarius is the first of two full moons in Aquarius in a row. The resolution of what this full moon brings up will not be seen until after the double full moon in Aquarius on August 22nd, 2021.

WHERE IS THIS FULL MOON HAPPENING IN YOUR CHART?

SUN/RISING SIGN	ASTROLOGICAL HOUSE
Aries	11th house
Taurus	10th house
Gemini	9th house
Cancer	8th house
Leo	7th house
Virgo	6th house
Libra	5th house
Scorpio	4th house
Sagittarius	3rd house
Capricorn	2nd house
Aquarius	1st house
Pisces	12th house

Look to page 11 for the definition of each house.

FULL MOON RITUAL

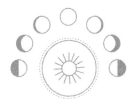

MOONLIGHT DANCING

This full moon, you are invited to spend some time dancing under the moonlight. This is a great way to move emotional energy and bring a lightness to this intense full moon, while also providing an opportunity to come into relationship with your own inner Shadow.

Open sacred space (see page 21). Put on some music and spend time dancing in the moonlight, either outside or inside beside a window where you can see the moonlight. If you aren't able to see the moonlight (because it's overcast, you aren't able to see the light from inside, etc) you can energetically connect with the moonlight through your awareness.

After you've spent some time dancing, you are invited to imagine your Shadow self outside of your physical body, and dance with your Shadow self. Notice any thoughts or feelings that come up for you as you're dancing with your Shadow.

Once you feel complete with your moonlight dance, close sacred space (see page 23).

LUGHNASADH

LUGHNASADH

Lughnasadh (Celtic) – Lammas (Anglo-Saxon) meaning 'loaf mass'
Midway point between Summer Solstice and Autumn Equinox

KEY LUGHNASADH PORTAL DATES

Traditional celebration date: August 1st
Solar Lughnasadh: August 7th, 2021 (12:00am Pacific)
Lunar Lughnasadh: August 22nd, 2021 (5am PST)

THEMES

Harvesting the fruits of our labors, assessment,
integration, discernment, abundance

SYMBOLS

Grain Mother, corn, bread, cauldron of plenty,
gold, Wicker Man, horses, John Barleycorn

HERBS, PLANTS & FLOWERS

Wheat, corn, barley, heather, sunflower,
yarrow, marigold, poppy

TRADITIONS

Neid fire, harvesting, feasting, making corn dolls, giving
thanks, dancing, travel, games, fairs and festivals,
mead, cider, beer, whiskey

ARCHETYPES

The Grain Goddess & God

The celebration of Lughnasadh is the first of three harvest festivals, the second taking place at the Autumn Equinox and the third at Samhain. The festivities would have begun when the harvests were gathered and the hunting parties had safely returned, which would have likely been around the August full moon. In the Irish Celtic tradition, Lugh is a god from the Tuatha Dé Danann, and although the festival is named after him, it is in actual fact to honor his foster mother Tailtiu, a goddess who is said to have brought agricultural farming to Ireland. Together, Lugh and Tailtiu invite us to shine our brightest and be generous with our bounty.

Above all, this is a festival that celebrates the god and goddess of the grain, as the Earth Mother who nourishes her children and the Grain God who sacrifices himself for his people. Grains and cereals like corn and barley were fundamental to the lives of our ancient ancestors, and so these crops held great significance.

Corn dollies were made, sometimes dressed in ribbons, and hung above fireplaces. Some corn dolls would have been made from the last sheaf and held a smaller corn doll inside to represent the next year's unborn harvest. A large Wicker Man was also sometimes created which was ceremonially burned.

Great feasts were held in communities and people would travel far and wide to enjoy the last days of summer.

Fairs and trading would have been an important part of the Lughnasadh celebrations, which included business transactions of all kinds as well as horse races, horse fairs, and ritual games. People would have enjoyed drinking beer, cider and whiskey from the previous year's harvest and there would have been dancing and merriment all around. Another important symbol is the cauldron of plenty, which is an ancient symbol from mythology that represents the abundance of Mother Earth's womb of creation.

Lughnasadh marks the beginning of the noticeable descent of the sun into the darkness of winter. Like so many of the Celtic festivals, this festival holds the energies of duality. On one hand, this is a time of merriment, feasting, drinking and games, and on the other hand, it's a time for taking stock, assessing the summer's harvest and making preparations for the colder months to come. Metaphorically, it's a time to ask ourselves, "What have we created and cultivated? What worked well and what didn't?"

IRISH SODA BREAD
LUGHNASADH RECIPE

Ingredients:

- 360 ml (1.5 cups) of buttermilk
- 2 cups (250g) of whole wheat flour
- 2 cups (250g) plain flour
- 1 tsp baking soda
- 1 tbsp caraways seeds
- 1 tbsp poppy seeds

DUTCH OVEN INSTRUCTIONS

Preheat oven to 475˚F (250˚C).

Once the oven is preheated, put the dutch oven into the oven with the lid to heat for 30 minutes.

Cut a square piece of 15" x 15" parchment paper and lightly grease.

Mix all the dry ingredients together and make a well in the center.

Add the buttermilk and mix it in lightly and quickly and form into a solid ball.

On a lightly floured surface, flatten the dough into a round loaf about 1 inch thick (2.5 cm). As you roll the loaf, be sure to keep moving the loaf so it doesn't stick to the counter top.

Once the loaf is round and flat, cut a large cross into the surface.

Transfer the loaf to the parchment paper.

Take the dutch oven out of the oven, remove the lid and carefully transfer the parchment paper with the loaf into the dutch oven. Use a wooden spoon to press down the edges.

Cut another square piece of 15" x 15" parchment paper, scrunch it into a ball and wet it with water from the tap, then stretch the parchment paper flat over the top of the dutch oven. Cut the excess parchment paper away from the dutch oven. Put on the lid, and place in the oven.

Bake for 30 minutes with the lid on, then take the lid off and bake for an additional 10 minutes.

Pierce the center with a thick skewer to check that it has cooked through (the skewer should come out clean).

Let cool for 15 minutes then wrap in a cloth to keep it soft until required.

NON-DUTCH OVEN INSTRUCTIONS

Preheat the oven to 375°F (190°C).

Cut a square piece of 15" x 15" parchment paper and lightly grease.

Mix all the dry ingredients together and make a well in the center.

Add the buttermilk and mix it in lightly and quickly and form into a solid ball.

On a lightly floured surface flatten the dough into a round loaf about 1 inch thick (2.5 cm). As you roll the loaf, be sure to keep moving the loaf so it doesn't stick to the counter top.

Once the loaf is round and flat, cut a large cross into the surface.

Transfer the loaf to the parchment paper.

Transfer the parchment paper onto a baking tray and place in the oven.

Bake for 40 minutes.

Pierce the center with a thick skewer to check that it has cooked through (the skewer should come out clean).

Let cool for 15 minutes then wrap in a cloth to keep it soft until required.

LUGHNASADH ASTROLOGY
AUGUST 1ST

PRIMARY INFLUENCE

Leo (Classical) - Og. (Celtic)

THEMES

Passion and desire
Manifestation
Discipline
Decision making

ASTROLOGY READING

On this day, the sun is in Leo and we will see a grand trine in fire again, but this time with the sun/Mercury conjunction trining the South Node as well as Chiron. In Celtic astrology, Og (Leo) is ruled by Grian (the sun) as in classical astrology, and is also connected to the star Uaithne (Lyra), which is one of the brightest stars in the summer sky.

Og carries the multidimensional, lyrical energies of Uaithne, which is symbolized by the harp, and desires to be seen and celebrated fully. Og also represents acts, facts, actions and decisions for action, which align with the energies of Lughnasadh, inviting us to make decisive action to prepare for the winter months ahead.

At this time, Saturn will be opposing the sun/Mercury conjunction at exactly 10 degrees. This is significant because even though a grand trine in fire activates our passion and our desire to manifest, Saturn asks to bring discipline and order into it, and that is exactly what we are going to be feeling at this time. Saturn will place restrictions on the expansion that we feel we need, or in a more simple way, he will be reminding us of the element of time, because he is the Lord of Time, as we continue to move forward in the year. As the days are getting significantly shorter at this time, it's important to remember to assess where we are at and see if we are prepared for the next phase. These things require maturity and discipline and that is what Saturn is asking the sun and Mercury in Leo to pay attention to.

AUGUST 8TH
NEW MOON IN LEO

6:51AM PST

PRIMARY INFLUENCE

Leo (Classical) - Og. (Celtic)

THEMES

Shining our light bright
The spiritual pioneer
Speaking our minds
Wisdom

ASTROLOGY READING

When we arrive at the new moon in Leo, the energy changes dramatically. This moon will be conjunct Mercury forming a Leo stellium in the sky. We will want to shine our light, we will want to be seen, we will desire to be valued and not taken for granted. Mercury will help us express ourselves without fear and draw attention to ourselves.

In Celtic astrology, Og (Leo) is represented by the harp and is connected with Uaithne, the alpha star of Lyra who is one of the brightest stars in the summer sky, so this is a natural time to express yourself in multidimensional ways. This is especially enhanced by the continued energies of Lughnasadh, where Lugh invites us to shine our brightest, as he is a master craftsman in the mythologies. The moon will also be trining Chiron, the wounded healer, and we may feel insecure. But with Neptune sextiling Pluto we will feel like spiritual pioneers who are unafraid to challenge the accepted way of thinking and doing things. This sextile is making a Yod to the moon pointing a finger at the resolution of this energy.

The resolution of this energy is to speak our mind, say what we want to say, show off our brightness and anchor the inner light. Neptune sextile Pluto has the potential to bring prophecies to light, and has the potential to activate powerful healing for humanity as a whole. With Mars in Virgo during this moon, set your intentions on how you can shine brightly but also remember to pay attention to the details and stay practical about the decisions you make in your life.

This is mirroried in Celtic astrology with Ech (Virgo) representing the constellation of the judge, inviting us to make our decisions wisely to create the best outcome. These themes of analysis and self-reflection are also very relevant to the continued energies of Lughnasadh as we ask ourselves, "What have we created and cultivated this harvest season? What worked well and what didn't?"

WHERE IS THIS NEW MOON HAPPENING IN YOUR CHART?

SUN/RISING SIGN	ASTROLOGICAL HOUSE
Aries	5lh house
Taurus	4th house
Gemini	3rd house
Cancer	2nd house
Leo	1st house
Virgo	12th house
Libra	11th house
Scorpio	10th house
Sagittarius	9th house
Capricorn	8th house
Aquarius	7th house
Pisces	6th house

Look to page 11 for the definition of each house.

NEW MOON RITUAL

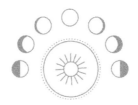

FIRE RITUAL

Our connection with fire is so ancient, so simple, and so sacred. We would not have survived without its warmth, and yet we are the only animal who has learned how to make it. There is something magical and mysterious about our relationship with fire that goes beyond words.

This new moon I invite you to tap into this sacred connection. If you have the opportunity, make a fire, or otherwise use a candle and imagine that you're sitting by a great fire. Write on a piece of paper something that you'd like to let go of during the next moon cycle, and an intention you'd like to call in, then burn the paper in the fire.

PRIMARY INFLUENCE

Aquarius (Classical) - Fii. (Celtic)

THEMES

A last call to action
Future focused intentions
The desire for a better future
A new beginning

ASTROLOGY READING

This is a very powerful double full moon at 29 degrees of Aquarius. Since July 20th 2020, there has been a phenomenon happening with the new and full moons. A new moon is a conjunction between the sun and the moon, and a full moon is an opposition from the sun to the moon. The new and full moons always align with the zodiacal dualities or opposite signs.

Usually, the sun will enter a zodiac sign, and soon after, as the moon conjuncts the sun, we will see a new moon in that sign. Two weeks later, as the moon travels through the zodiac and begins to oppose the sun, we will see a full moon in the opposite sign that the sun is in.

On July 20th 2020, we had a new moon solar eclipse in Cancer on the Summer Solstice, a full moon lunar eclipse in Capricorn two weeks later, followed by a second new moon in Cancer two weeks after that. Since then, each time the sun has moved into a new zodiac sign, the moon has opposed the sun before conjuncting it. We've been seeing the full moons (the sun-moon opposition) arrive before the new moons (the sun-moon conjunction). This has forced us to feel the completion energy of the moon cycle expressed as a full moon, before the initiatory energies of a new moon phase, during each zodiac season.

On this double full moon in Aquarius, the cycle will reset and we will once again return to the "normal" way of seeing the new moon arriving before the full moon, during each zodiac season,

It's almost as if for the last year or so we have been living in an alternate reality or a different dimension. Many people talk about the Earth ascending into the 5th dimension and I believe that during this past year we have felt that shift.

This moon is conjunct Jupiter and Saturn in Aquarius at the last degree (the 29th degree), which makes this moon a last call to take action. In this case, this moon will bring in many mysteries to light, exposing us to revolutionary energies and future thinking. We will feel like we are witnessing events that are out of the ordinary, unique, and maybe even prophesied about.

The only three planets that are direct at this point are Mars, Venus and Mercury, and Mars and Mercury are conjunct in the sign Virgo. Virgo is about being of service to the world. Our desire for a better future will be driven by the need to help humanity rise above the darkness, and our minds will be activated by a desire to be practical and analyze every detail that is being presented and coming to light.

As Fii (Aquarius) teaches in Celtic astrology, our personal (and collective) leadership is needed to gain any kind of spiritual reward. This is about focusing on the details and holding yourself rooted in your thoughts and actions. This moon officially ends the flipped cycle of the moons we have been experiencing for a year now. It's the culmination of everything that has happened, since that double new moon in Cancer and now a new cycle begins.

WHERE IS THIS FULL MOON HAPPENING IN YOUR CHART?

SUN/RISING SIGN	ASTROLOGICAL HOUSE
Aries	11th house
Taurus	10th house
Gemini	9th house
Cancer	8th house
Leo	7th house
Virgo	6th house
Libra	5th house
Scorpio	4th house
Sagittarius	3rd house
Capricorn	2nd house
Aquarius	1st house
Pisces	12th house

Look to page 11 for the definition of each house.

FULL MOON
RITUAL

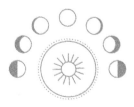

JOURNALING PRACTICE

With the continued energies of the harvest and the celebration of Lunar Lughnasadh, this is a beautiful opportunity to pause and reflect on your own metaphorical harvest. Here are a few journaling questions for you to reflect on this full moon:

What am I harvesting in my life right now?

What worked well during the active time of the year, and what didn't?

In what areas of my life do I need to bring softness, forgiveness, or compassion?

SEPTEMBER 6TH
NEW MOON IN VIRGO

5:52PM PST

PRIMARY INFLUENCE

Virgo (Classical) - Ech. (Celtic)

THEMES

Anchoring the light
Channeling from the spiritual realm
Purification
Strong will

ASTROLOGY READING

It's so refreshing to finally see the Virgo new moon come before the Pisces full moon. A new alignment has begun in the sky. The Virgo and Pisces duality are all about anchoring the higher dimensions into this space time reality. It's about calling in the messages from the divine and living them out here in the 3D.

This Virgo new moon is about taking passionate action towards healing our bodies and finding joy in our daily lives. Virgo is about purifying ourselves. In Celtic astrology Ech (Virgo) is the last sign in the astrological year and is connected with the 12th house, presenting an important opportunity to purify ourselves before moving into the next cycle. If we have been living in alignment with who we truly are and our higher purpose, we will be judged with "perfect fairness" and rewarded with bounties that are not necessarily for the world to see, but are felt deeply and experienced on a personal level.

There is also a Virgo stellium in the sky with the sun, moon and Mars. Mars is making an exact trine to Pluto at 24 degrees of Capricorn. Mars trine Pluto is an intense force to be reckoned with. Whenever Mars and Pluto come together for any purpose, they activate each other's powers. Mars moves into action while Pluto destroys that which no longer serves. This is about becoming strong willed, determined to succeed, courageous and confident in life. With the moon making a trine to Uranus, expect the unexpected because Uranus likes to bring in surprises.

Venus, in its ruling sign of Libra, is going through an interesting dilemma. She is both trining Jupiter who brings joy into her life, but also squaring Pluto which creates drama. This is like Venus trying to balance the light and the dark, the good and the bad, the yin and the yang. She is reminding us that life is a constant balancing act.

In Celtic astrology Ind (Libra) is symbolized by the hoop of life, which holds the entire balance of life. What comes, goes; what begins, ends; where there is light, there is also darkness; where there is life, there is also death. In the end, everything is embraced in the hoop of life, which is an important lesson to remember at this time. Last but not least, we have Neptune opposing this moon and we may feel insecurities come up or we may find ourselves being self-critical. We must remember where our courage comes from, and it's through the connection to Mars that we will find our strength.

WHERE IS THIS NEW MOON HAPPENING IN YOUR CHART?

SUN/RISING SIGN	ASTROLOGICAL HOUSE
Aries	6th house
Taurus	5th house
Gemini	4th house
Cancer	3rd house
Leo	2nd house
Virgo	1st house

SUN/RISING SIGN (CONTINUED)	ASTROLOGICAL HOUSE (CONTINUED)
Libra	12th house
Scorpio	11th house
Sagittarius	10th house
Capricorn	9th house
Aquarius	8th house
Pisces	7th house

Look to page 11 for the definition of each house.

NEW MOON
RITUAL

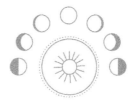

STRAW BRAID OFFERING

In this ritual you are invited to learn how to make a straw braid. You are invited to make one braid as an offering to the land that you live on, and one braid for your seasonal altar.

First, prepare the straw by soaking it in warm water until it's pliable enough to braid, fold, twist or bend without splitting or cracking. Use a piece of tough thread to tie four straws together with a clove hitch just under the heads. (If you're not familiar with the clove hitch knot, you can find a demonstration in Additional Resources at the back of this book.)

Braid the straw until you have about 8cm/3 inches of straw left. Bring the four straws up to meet each other, and tie firmly at the end of the braided section with another clove hitch.

Bring this tie down to meet the other tie just under the heads, to form a loop of braided straw, and tie the two together. Spread the wheat ears out between the wheat stalks and allow to dry flat, preferably under a weight.

When you dry out the braid, you can clip the stalk ends decoratively, and add a ribbon bow or a small sprig of dried flowers.

SEPTEMBER 20TH
FULL MOON IN PISCES

4:55PM PST

PRIMARY INFLUENCE

Pisces (Classical) - Ict. (Celtic)

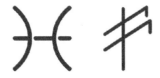

THEMES

The mystical
The universe
Crown chakra activation
Discovering what is hidden

ASTROLOGY READING

The Full moon in Pisces takes us to the world of Neptune and the 12th house which rules divine connection, our relationship to God/Source, our psychic and intuitive powers, the unknown, trusting in the universe, and receiving downloads from higher dimensions.

This is also mirrored in Celtic astrology with Ict (Pisces) being connected with the invisible realms. This moon will also be conjunct Neptune in Pisces which will expand this energy.

The moon will be trining the South Node which brings up the past, and the moon will also be opposing Mars and the sun. Mars is actually activating our passion but when Mars is in the sign of Libra, which is its detriment, we have to be careful about being wishy washy or unable to make decisions or make up our mind about stuff.

This moon at the last degrees of Pisces is opening up our crown chakra so that we may receive a beautiful message, and the grand trine in air will activate our conscious awareness and intellectual mind to help us make sense of the messages. This moon is a deep dive into the unknown to discover things that are hidden.

WHERE IS THIS FULL MOON HAPPENING IN YOUR CHART?

SUN/RISING SIGN	ASTROLOGICAL HOUSE
Aries	12th house
Taurus	11th house
Gemini	10th house
Cancer	9th house
Leo	8th house
Virgo	7th house
Libra	6th house
Scorpio	5th house
Sagittarius	4th house
Capricorn	3rd house
Aquarius	2nd house
Pisces	1st house

Look to page 11 for the definition of each house.

FULL MOON
RITUAL

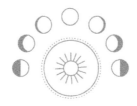

LUNAR ELIXIR

Making sacred water under the light of the full moon (what I call a Lunar Elixir) is a simple and fun practice to honor Grandmother Moon.

You will need: A bottle, jar or dish, essential oils, fresh herbs or flowers of your choice, and water which may be from a Holy Well, river, or your home tap.

Gather the essential oils and fresh herbs or flowers and put them into your bottle, jar or dish. Add the water and a few drops of essential oil. Leave your bottle, jar or dish outside under the light of the full moon. Don't worry if it's cloudy, it will still be charged by the moon's energies. Ideally leave it out from dusk until dawn (the whole night).

Now you have your Lunar Elixir, make sure to keep it in the fridge and use it within the next few days (before the fresh herbs and flowers start to deteriorate and create bacteria in the water). Please note that it's not intended for consumption. You can use the elixir to anoint yourself during ritual by dipping your fingers into the water and bringing the water to your mind, heart and womb space to cultivate a feeling of sacred sovereignty in your body. You can use your elixir in a bath, where you might like to imagine this special sacred water washing away what no longer serves you while setting a new intention. If you have any left then offer this to the earth to show gratitude for the land you live on.

AUTUMN
EQUINOX

AUTUMN EQUINOX

Mabon (Celtic) - Alban Elued (Druid) - Michaelmas (Christian)
Equal balance of light and darkness

EQUINOX PORTAL KEY DATES

Autumn Equinox: September 22nd, 2021
Equinox portal: September 21st - September 23rd

THEMES

Balance, harmony, beauty, letting go,
preparation, gratitude, generosity,
relationships

SYMBOLS

Mother Earth, harvest, dragon, roots, apples,
leaves, honey, mead, cider, Horned God

HERBS, PLANTS & FLOWERS

Elderberry, scullcap, rosehips,
pumpkin seeds, dried apples

TRADITIONS

Fermenting, medicine making, feasting, giving thanks,
collecting leaves, space clearing

ARCHETYPES

Earth Mother Queen and the Horned God

The equinoxes are a time of balance, when the light and darkness stand in equal balance. This is a time for connecting with the harmonious and beautiful aspects of life. It's a time of coming together, giving thanks for the second harvest, and all of Mother Earth's bounty. It's a time for rest and celebration, after the hard work of gathering the crops. At this time, the ancestors saw the Earth Mother Queen, who is sovereign Spirit of the Land, stand before her people with the full bounty of her harvest.

Both Spring and Autumn equinoxes are times to celebrate the energies of the dragon; in springtime we celebrate the dragon energies rising within us, and in Autumn we celebrate the dragon energies descending and bringing us down into our roots. The energies of the stag are also present at this time with hunting season and as the Horned God walks among the forests.

At this moment in the wheel of the year, our energies turn towards completing things, reaping what we've sown, typing up loose ends, getting organized for winter, and preparing for our journey into our inner realms, which activate during winter. It's a time to get grounded, get rooted, and be practical. Our ancestors would have been making medicines, fermenting vegetables, organizing grains, and generally taking stock.

This was a time when communities came together to help one another and make sure that everyone had what they needed before the months of winter. Autumn Equinox is a time when the sun's power is quickly waning. While this is very much a busy time for taking care of matters in the material realm, it's also important to take stock of our inner realms as we begin to turn our attention inwards. At this time we're harvesting the seeds we have sown (physically and metaphorically) and also coming face to face with the Autumn-time energies of letting go. With the Celtic year coming to an end at Samhain (October 31st) this is a time to reflect on the year gone by, to forgive ourselves for mistakes we might have made, the thing we wish we'd done or didn't do, and the build inner resilience for the regeneration and rebirthing process we'll experience through the winter.

There is so much beauty to receive with all of the energies of Autumn time, as we reflect on our relationship with all of life and enjoy the last of the warmth before the winter comes. This is a time to give thanks for being alive and to the wheel of life that is forever turning. In ancient times when wintertime often meant loss of life in communities, this was also a time to cherish loved ones and the gift of the present moment. In particular, this is a beautiful moment to listen to the wisdom of the elders in our lives.

BAKED APPLE PUDDING AUTUMN EQUINOX RECIPE

Ingredients:

- 4 tbsp (50g) butter
- 600 ml milk
- 4 tbsp plain flour
- 3 eggs
- 3 small to medium sweet apples, peeled and cored
- 1 tbsp maple syrup
- 1 tsp vanilla extract
- ¼ tsp ground nutmeg
- Caster sugar to serve
- Cinnamon to serve

Preheat the oven to 350°F (180°C).

Use about a third of the butter to grease a shallow ovenproof dish.

Core, peel and cut the apples into thick slices.

Gradually whisk a little of the milk into the flour to make a smooth paste.

Beat the eggs into the mixture, add the remaining milk, and add the vanilla extract.

Pour the custard mixture into the dish and arrange the apples in the dish.

Sprinkle the nutmeg over the top of the dish and lightly drizzle the maple syrup over top.

Cut the remaining butter into small pieces and dot over the apples.

Bake for 60 - 75 minutes until the custard mixture is risen and lightly browned, and the apples are cooked.

Sprinkle caster sugar and cinnamon over the finished pudding to serve.

AUTUMN EQUINOX ASTROLOGY
SEPTEMBER 22ST

PRIMARY INFLUENCE

Libra (Classical) - Ind. (Celtic)

THEMES

Balance
Reflecting on the past
Higher perspective
Endings

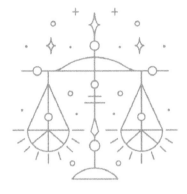

ASTROLOGY READING

The sun moves into the sign of Libra, with Ind (Libra) representing the new astrological year in Celtic astrology. Ind (Libra) is associated with the first house in Celtic astrology, however there is something important to note here. The first house in Celtic astrology is actually associated with loss, limit and the end result (in other words, endings).

This may seem backwards to the modern mind, but this gives us a very important clue to how the Celtic ancestors of old regarded the wheel of life. In the Celtic mind, we have to die to be reborn. Things have to end in order to begin. It is thought that the Celts regarded night time as the beginning of a new day, rather than the dawn. Here at Ind (Libra), we see the end falling into the beginning rather than one definitive moment, like the symbol of the snake eating its own tail. Ind is represented by the symbol of the ring, symbolic of the wheel of the year where we have come full circle, and is ruled by Riia (Venus) who helps us to see the beauty in life, just as Libra is ruled by Venus in classical astrology.

The sun in Libra at this time is also conjunct Mars. Internally our desire is to find balance in our lives as well as to focus on our relationships. The sun will be making a grand trine in the sky with the North Node and Saturn, all in air signs. This air grand trine will activate our higher minds and help us to communicate clearly as well as open our minds to a higher perspective. The sun, Mars and Saturn will also be sextiling the South Node, creating what is known as a Kyte in astrology. When a Kyte is formed we receive clear information about where to focus our energy.

The focus of this day is to look back at the past and reflect on everything that has happened in the past year or so. The Nodes will be switching signs soon and the energy of Gemini and Sagittarius will come to a completion.

Reflection is an important part of growth and forward movement, and with all of the retrogrades that we've been seeing, reflection has been a recurring theme for a while.

OCTOBER 6TH
NEW MOON IN LIBRA

4AM PST

PRIMARY INFLUENCE

Libra (Classical) - Ind. (Celtic)

THEMES

Forward movement begins
Balance and beauty
Justice and fairness
Relationships

ASTROLOGY READING

On this day, we will begin to see the planets start to come out of retrograde. The first planet that goes direct on the day of this new moon is Pluto. Things will start to feel like they are beginning to move forward again. The moon will be in a Libra stellium with the sun, Mars and Mercury.

This combination of planets in the sign of Libra asks us to be logical, to see the beauty in everything, to seek balance in our lives, to be fair and focus on our relationships. With Mercury retrograde in Libra we will be doing a lot of thinking about whether we have been fair in relationships or not, and whether we have found the balance we've been looking for in our lives.

In Celtic astrology, Ind (Libra) represents the sign of perfect fairness and judgement, so we will naturally be analytical of ourselves at this time, but it's important to remember not to be overly judgmental of ourselves. We will want to look at all sides of the equation before making up our minds about anything. This energy can also create indecisiveness because Libra doesn't always know how to make up its mind. Chiron is also challenging us to heal any codependency wounds we might have, and feelings of not knowing who we are because we lose ourselves in our relationships sometimes. The moon will also be making a trine to Saturn which will encourage us to find balance between our professional and personal lives. With Venus ruling this moon and conjunct with the South Node, this is going to feel like we are being forced to look at our past relationships to find the places where much deeper healing is needed. You may notice by this point in the year that you have outgrown some people in your life, and in some cases you must choose to move on.

WHERE IS THIS NEW MOON HAPPENING IN YOUR CHART?

SUN/RISING SIGN	ASTROLOGICAL HOUSE
Aries	7th house
Taurus	6th house
Gemini	5th house
Cancer	4th house
Leo	3rd house
Virgo	2nd house
Libra	1st house
Scorpio	12th house
Sagittarius	11th house
Capricorn	10th house
Aquarius	9th house
Pisces	8th house

Look to page 11 for the definition of each house.

NEW MOON
RITUAL

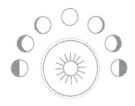

JOURNALING PRACTICE

At this time of year the light and darkness are in balance, symbolising the dualistic nature of life, mirrored in Libra's energies of balance and beauty, harmony and justice. In your journal, spend some time reflecting on these questions.

How do I honor the old ways while living a modern life?

How do I hold humility in one hand and power in the other?

How can I invite more beauty into my daily life at this time?

OCTOBER 20TH
FULL MOON IN ARIES

8AM PST

PRIMARY INFLUENCE

Aires (Classical) - Arb. (Celtic)

THEMES

Self identity
Self image
Independence vs. relationships
Drive and desire to initiate

ASTROLOGY READING

By the time we reach this full moon in Aries we will have only 3 planets retrograde. Saturn, Jupiter and Mercury will have gone direct. However, this full moon is going to be T-squared by Pluto which will bring to light issues regarding our personal identity and the self-image that we hide from the rest of the world.

This is a battle between our independence and our desire to be in relationship. This is about finding the balance between the two, but also feeling free to be ourselves. A full moon in Aries activates our drive and desire to initiate things, to move forward in life with enthusiasm and courage.

This is mirrored in Celtic astrology with Arb (Aires) represented by the fiery ram, and associations with storm energy and the sparking of energy. I think it's beautiful that we end our journal with this full moon, which opens up a whole new portal for our futures.

What will be our next move? How much have we learned through this process? Are we ready to begin anew?

WHERE IS THIS FULL MOON HAPPENING IN YOUR CHART?

SUN/RISING SIGN	ASTROLOGICAL HOUSE
Aries	1st house
Taurus	12th house
Gemini	11th house
Cancer	10th house
Leo	9th house
Virgo	8th house
Libra	7th house
Scorpio	6th house
Sagittarius	5th house
Capricorn	4th house
Aquarius	3rd house
Pisces	2nd house

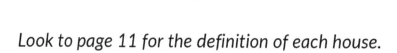

Look to page 11 for the definition of each house.

FULL MOON RITUAL

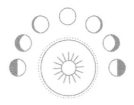

DIVINATION RITUAL

Divination is an ancient practice used all over the world as a way of interpreting meaning and the will of the gods/spirit. This is a shamanic practice that was used by the druids during Celtic times for prophesying, decision making, and seeing the truth of any given situation in the present moment. Divination can be done with bones, berries, sticks, stones, smoke, water, clouds, animal patterns, bird song, symbols and more. For this ritual, you are invited to use a bowl of water and an herb or plant of your choice. You will also need a candle. The idea is to gaze into the bowl of herbs and water and look for visions, symbols and messages to be shown through the patterns the herbs create.

Open sacred space (see page 21). Please note that this ritual is best done in a darkened space. Place the bowl of water in front of you, with the candle behind the bowl so that it lights up the surface of the water. Call upon any spiritual or ancestral guides to help open your mind to the divination practice and receive messages that will give you deeper insight into your life. Close your eyes, connect to your breath and quiet your mind.

Place your herbs into your bowl of water. Begin gazing into the bowl of water. Soften your gaze. Open your awareness to the patterns of the herbs and connect with any visions, symbols or messages that want to come through, or you may experience feelings or sensations. There's no wrong way to do divination. Once you feel complete with the divination, you can record any visions or messages you received in your journal. Thank your spiritual and ancestral guides. Close sacred space (see page 23).

THANK YOU FOR TAKING THIS
JOURNEY, BEAUTIFUL SOUL...

BLESSINGS

CONNECT WITH JAI

Instagram: @channelforgrace
Facebook: @channelforgrace.jai.gobind
YouTube: Channel for Grace
Website: www.channelforgrace.guru

Jai Gobind is an intuitive, writer, songstress, jewelry designer, astrologer and the founder and creator of Eagle Star Yoga LLC, the Eagle Star Sisterhood, Eagle Star Jewels and Channel for Grace.

She runs a Moon Goddess Training, a beginners astrology course called Aquarian Astrology and has just finished another online course called Woman and the Moon. She offers astrology webinars and private astrology and tarot readings.

Through her work, Jai Gobind guides you to connect deeply with your heart space, find the courage to trust your intuition and align with the healing and sustaining life force of the universe. On her YouTube channel (Channel for Grace) you will find monthly moon, zodiac and collective ascension astrology, as well as new moon and full moon ceremonies for spiritual evolution.

CONNECT WITH TARA

Instagram: @tarawild
Facebook: www.facebook.com/ms.tara.wild
YouTube: Tara Wild
Website: www.tara-wild.com

Tara is a womxn's educator, storyteller, healer and songstress. She's been on a journey of remembering and reclamation for the past ten years, following the Celtic traditions of old, honoring the sacred scriptures left in her blood and bones.

She offers an online monthly membership called Wild & Wise, connecting womxn to the ancient, feminine wisdom of the Celtic ancestors and bringing it into modern life. She also offers 1-1 ancestral healing sessions to release grief, pain and trauma, which is inspired by the ancient Irish practice of keening. She also has a variety of guided journeys available for download, a podcast series called 'Dreaming the Ancestors', and a vibrant Facebook group.

Tara journeys to the Celtic Isles regularly for pilgrimage and is an avid photographer. She's a storyteller, entrepreneur, and has created and directed films for the past ten years. She lives in the mountains of Colorado with her husband and two dogs.

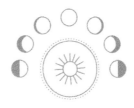

ADDITIONAL RESOURCES

Brigid's cross/St Bridget's cross making tutorial:
https://youtu.be/WErPG3DiT24

Making a clove hitch notch demonstration:
https://www.animatedknots.com/clove-hitch-knot-using-loops

The High Man - full documentary about ancient Ireland's myths and
monuments:
https://youtu.be/ALcP1o2EUio

The Fabrication of 'Celtic' Astrology article by Peter Berresford Ellis:
http://cura.free.fr/xv/13ellis2.html

Celtic Astrology from the Druids to the Middle Ages
by M.G. Boutet (book)